Battle Orders • 6

The American Expeditionary Forces in World War I

John F Votaw

Consultant Editor Dr Duncan Anderson • *Series editors* Marcus Cowper and Nikolai Bogdanovic

First published in Great Britain in 2005 by Osprey Publishing,
Midland House, West Way, Botley, Oxford OX2 0PH, UK
44-02 23rd St, Suite 219, Long Island City, NY 11101, USA
Email: info@ospreypublishing.com

Transferred to digital print on demand 2010

First published 2005
2nd impression 2008

Printed and bound by Cadmus Communications, USA

A CIP catalog record for this book is available from the British Library

ISBN: 978 1 84176 622 5

Editorial by Ilios Publishing, Oxford, UK (www.iliospublishing.com)
Design by Bounford.com, Royston, UK
Maps by Bounford.com, Royston, UK
Index by David Worthington
Originated by The Electronic Page Company, Cwmbran, UK
Typeset in Adobe Garamond and Univers

FOR A CATALOG OF ALL BOOKS PUBLISHED BY
OSPREY MILITARY AND AVIATION PLEASE CONTACT:

Osprey Direct, c/o Random House Distribution Center,
400 Hahn Road, Westminster, MD 21157
Email: uscustomerservice@ospreypublishing.com

Osprey Direct, The Book Service Ltd, Distribution Centre,
Colchester Road, Frating Green, Colchester,
Essex, CO7 7DW
Email: customerservice@ospreypublishing.com

www.ospreypublishing.com

Acknowledgments
I have believed for some time that the history of the American
Expeditionary Forces in World War I was the story of a remarkable
achievement of intellect, organizational skill, and raw determination
on the part of the American military establishment. Although blunders
in execution and bureaucratic snaggling took some of the luster off
that achievement, the work of General John J. Pershing still stands
as an important instructive chapter in American military history. The
scholarship of others has made it possible for me to make this small
contribution of illuminating the AEF for the large, non-academic group
of readers. Professors Edward M. Coffman, Russell F. Weigley,
Allan R. Millett and others have blazed a well-marked trail through the
literature of World War 1. Dr. Timothy K. Nenninger and his colleague
Mitchell Yockelson at the College Park, Maryland, facility of the
National Archives have provided immeasurable help in understanding
the documentary records of the AEF in their custody. My family and
friends have patiently, though anxiously watched the hatching of this
small book. My museum and library colleagues at the First Division
Museum at Cantigny and its collocated Colonel Robert R. McCormick
Research Center, particularly Eric Gillespie and Andrew Woods'
have helped find relevant materials in their very useful archival and photograph
collections. Finally, to my AEF friend Private Max Ottenfeld, a signal
wireman of the 18th Infantry Regiment now gone to his reward, well done
good and faithful soldier. To all, thank you. The remaining infelicities of
expression and any errors of fact and interpretation are mine alone.

Editor's note
Excerpt from *Memoirs of My Services In The World War, 1917-1918*
by George C. Marshall, Copyright (c) 1976 by Molly B. Winn. Reprinted
by permission of Houghton Mifflin Company. All rights reserved.

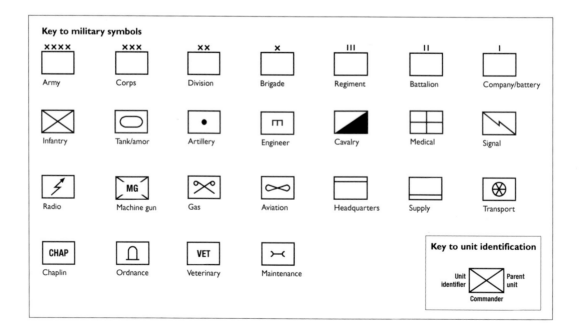

Key to military symbols

XXXX	XXX	XX	X	III	II	I
Army	Corps	Division	Brigade	Regiment	Battalion	Company/battery
Infantry	Tank/amor	Artillery	Engineer	Cavalry	Medical	Signal
Radio	Machine gun	Gas	Aviation	Headquarters	Supply	Transport
Chaplin	Ordnance	Veterinary	Maintenance			

Key to unit identification

Unit identifier — Parent unit — Commander

Contents

Introduction 4

Mission 7

Preparation for war 9
Training in the US • Training in France • Schools in France

Command, control, communication, and intelligence 19
Command and control • Communication • Intelligence

Organization 27
The AEF General Headquarters and staff • The First Army • I Corps
The division • The division infantry brigade • The division artillery brigade • The Air Service
The Tank Corps • The Services of Supply (SOS) • The engineers • Medical services
American Expeditionary Forces, North Russia; American Expeditionary Forces, Siberia;
American Forces in France; American Forces in Germany

Tactics 63
Cantigny: a regimental attack supported by the division
Soissons: a divisional attack as part of a French corps
The tactics of aerial combat • Tank tactics

Weapons and equipment 78
Equipment • Individual weapons • Automatic weapons • Artillery
Armored fighting vehicles • Rail and truck transport • Aircraft

Armistice, occupation, recovery, and demobilization 84

Retrospective 88

Chronology 90

Bibliography 91

Source notes 93

Index 95

Introduction

Unlike the British, French, and German armies prior to 1917, the United States Army did not have a permanent field army organization or an operational staff to support it. There were no combat divisions, army corps, or armies—only regiments. This is partly a consequence of the infrequency of US involvement in foreign wars requiring an expeditionary army and the navy to carry it to the theater of operations. It is also a result of the way that the American armed forces developed after the creation of the Republic at the end of the 18th century. Throughout its history the army, and to a lesser degree the navy, developed with two strong elements: a small but capable standing, professional force, and a "nation in arms" citizen force that mobilized as threats developed. Of the two, the latter force was more consistent with the values of a democratic

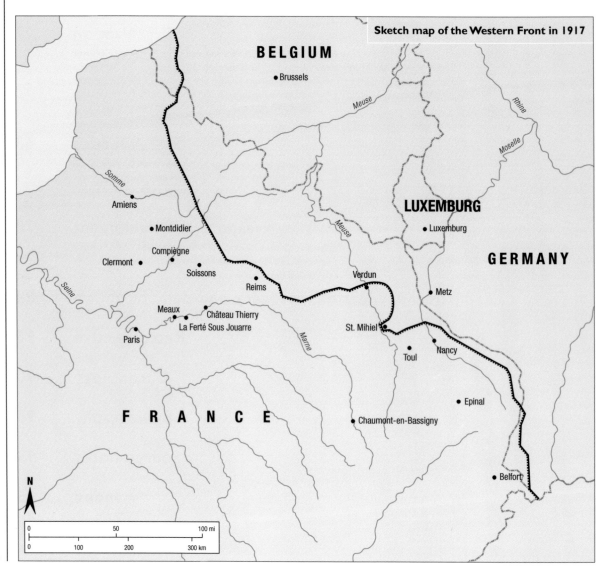

Sketch map of the Western Front in 1917

republic, but it also was harder to maintain professional competence within an exclusively conscripted or volunteer army. At the end of the Civil War in the United States, advocates for both approaches to maintaining an armed force argued their positions. Emory Upton, a veteran Union Army officer, wrote of a military policy for the United States that relied on a small, professional standing army that could be expanded in times of emergency. Others, notably John McAuley Palmer who was to serve in World War I, believed that the citizen army, or militia, could effectively protect

Officers of the 26th French Division, Chasseurs Alpins, who instructed the 1st Division at Gondrecourt, France, in the fall of 1917. (US Signal Corps, 80066)

the nation. The war with Mexico in 1846–48, the Civil War (1861–65), and the Spanish–American War (1898) were waged with mostly volunteer regiments. In 1887 *The Volunteer Soldier in America* by Major General John Logan, an Illinois veteran of the Civil War, argued against a standing regular army in favor of the volunteer citizen-soldier as the main line of defense for America. Although the wars waged by the United States in the 19th century were bloody and involved large field armies, it was not until World War I that the United States was confronted by modern technology combined with mass armies in an extremely large theater of operations.

In 1917 most American men of military age had not traveled far beyond the homes where they were raised. Many soldiers came from rural communities and had attained some secondary education. They certainly were not worldly or even cosmopolitan in their outlook. In many instances, their service in the army was their first group experience. African-Americans served in significant numbers, but their service was clouded partly by the prevailing racial discrimination of the era.

Some recent histories have argued that the arrival of two million largely untrained and untested American doughboys in France at the very time that European armies, including the German enemy, were on the wane, tipped the balance of victory to the Allies. This is only partly true, as no single factor produced Allied victory. It may also be said that the enormous sacrifices of the British and French field armies prevented a German victory before the spring of 1918. This hyper-national way of viewing the largest military involvement of nations in modern history up to that point does not explain the success of either the Allied nations or the American Expeditionary Forces. This short book presents the elements of the AEF that permitted rapid organization and training that ultimately led to its making a significant contribution to Allied victory in World War I.

Portrait of General John J. Pershing by John Doctoroff, oil on canvas, 30 by 24in., 1938, in the collections of the 1st Division Museum at Cantigny, Wheaton, Illinois. (FDM)

There are four distinct but interrelated phases in the development of the AEF as an effective fighting force. First, the successful mobilization and movement of units to the debarkation ports so that they could be transported to France efficiently was essential. Second, the reception at the French ports of arrival and smooth movement to the training areas in northeastern France had to be accomplished with minimal disruption to ongoing Allied operations. Third, the AEF had to be trained quickly and made ready for combat operations compatible with the needs of the Allied high command. And finally, the AEF had to develop increasingly effective systems of command, control, and support as its strength increased from divisions to armies. Throughout this progressive development, the high command of the AEF had to find ways to integrate its efforts with those of the other Allies while remaining politically independent and faithful to the intent of the American president, the US Congress, and the American people. All of this was achieved in a remarkably short time with minimum shortfalls. If the AEF did not win the war in France for the Allies, it certainly had a major part in making that victory possible.

Born in Missouri in 1860, John Joseph Pershing, first captain of his West Point class of 1886, was not the most apparent choice to command the AEF in France, but he was the best choice. Captain Pershing, a cavalry officer on duty in Japan as a military attaché, had been advanced to the rank of brigadier general in 1906 over many other more senior officers in the army. His father-in-law, Senator Francis Warren of Wyoming, assisted in bringing his son-in-law's name to the attention of those who could help him, then the chairman of the Senate Military Affairs Committee shepherded the appointment through the government bureaucracy. Pershing's assignment to command the 8th Infantry Brigade, first at the Presidio of San Francisco then in Texas in April 1914, was attended by the tragedy that forever changed his personal life. In August 1915, his family had been trapped and killed in a quarters fire at the Presidio. Only his six-year-old son Warren had survived. In 1916 he was appointed to head a punitive expedition into Mexico to find and capture Francisco "Pancho" Villa. In September 1916, President Woodrow Wilson promoted Pershing to major general. By this time the tall, good-humored "Spartan" general had made his mark with his superiors and the American public. The audience he had to persuade, however, were the Allied nations fighting in Europe.

The story of the AEF is mostly the story of the progressive development of a large field army and its many supporting organizations. Part of the story is the contribution of airpower and another part is the role of the US Navy in moving men and materiel to France. The former will be addressed in this book, but the latter is at the periphery, with the exception of the 4th Brigade, 2d Division (the Marine Brigade). The essence of an effective field army is the sum of trained and motivated soldiers, flexible and, resilient organization, inspired and competent leadership, appropriate doctrine and functional logistics. When the AEF landed in France not one of those elements was fully developed. The American field army was unprepared for combat. "Black Jack" Pershing dominated that situation as commander-in-chief of the AEF and imposed his personality, style and, some would say, his stubbornness, as he shaped and prepared his fighting forces to take their place in the line and in history. He was the forceful opponent of sloth, age, infirmity, and obstinacy. Pershing would accept no interference in his command prerogatives, and, as a result, some judged him as aloof and uncaring. The instrument he fashioned to bring the weight of the American nation to bear in France was powerful, potentially lethal, and often unwieldy. But one thing was absolutely certain: the AEF was General Pershing's army.

Since no effective staff system for the control of field operations and training of a large force existed in 1917, Pershing and his "coterie" created one from whole cloth. Most of those officers were graduates of the School of the Line and/or the Staff College at Fort Leavenworth, Kansas. The AEF staff controlled all American military activities in the theater of operations, except the work of the military attachés and others assigned to various missions and embassies. Intelligence staff work was a "stovepipe," or vertical system whereby the Military Intelligence Division of the War Department General Staff (WDGS) had a direct line to the G-2 (intelligence staff section) of the AEF, for matters of higher intelligence. Tactical intelligence that was immediately useful for continuing combat operations remained the purview of the field commanders. Dentistry, medicine, and nursing, although organized activities of the AEF, were handled in an ancillary way for most of the war in cooperative efforts with the French and British. The achievement of this imperfect system was all the more remarkable in that it worked, even if in a flawed way. All American divisions, with the exception of the Air Service, in France were infantry divisions of roughly 28,000 men and 6,600 animals each. A staff officer at General Headquarters AEF and operations units at army, corps, and division level represented the American Air Service.

Armies usually fight as they have trained. In most instances the armies of the World War I era had a solid base of doctrine that governed training and combat. In the case of the AEF, that tactical-operational doctrine was inchoate and largely untested in 1917. General Pershing wanted his army to fight in "open warfare" style. He knew what that meant and his major subordinate commanders and staff officers professed to know what he meant, but in action the AEF divisions fought mostly as their French, and in some cases British, trainers had taught them. The American soldiers, however, were imbued with an offensive spirit that often carried them forward in the face of withering fire from enemy machine guns, mortars, and artillery.

Beginning with Cantigny in May 1918, Belleau Wood in June, Soissons in July, St. Mihiel in September, and the Meuse–Argonne from late September to mid-November, the fighting divisions of the AEF sustained increasing casualties. By the time of the final campaign of the war, those divisions were infused with replacements to such an extent that the character of the original divisions had been changed. Many junior officers and noncommissioned officers had been killed, wounded, or promoted, leaving the AEF with a new training problem right in the midst of its sternest combat test. Pershing and others expected that the war would last well into 1919 before the Allies would finally prevail.

Mission

At the time President Woodrow Wilson asked the United States Congress to declare war on Germany and the other Central Powers on April 6, 1917, the US Army was a small provincial force recently engaged in coastal defense and field operations against Mexican irregulars. In May 1916 the army consisted of 65 regiments of infantry, 25 of cavalry, and 21 of artillery, with a total strength of 108,399 officers and men. The National Defense Act of 1916 had authorized a regular army of 175,000 soldiers in peacetime to be expanded to 286,000 in wartime. The National Guard was to be built up to 400,000 men and be supervised federally. The following year, on the threshold of America's entry into the war, the army had expanded by nearly four times, but still numbered under 500,000 men. This was the instrument to be wielded by the United States in forming its expeditionary forces for service in France. A new Secretary of War, Ohio lawyer and politician Newton D. Baker, and 19 officers to man the department's general staff seemed woefully inadequate to wage modern war.

When Major General John Pershing's forces were withdrawn from Mexico in February 1917, they had learned important lessons in transportation, logistics, and aviation, despite their failure to defeat Pancho Villa. At the moment of declaration of war, it was not clear that the United States intended to send a mass army to Europe. Some thought that the limited affront of the resumption of unrestricted submarine warfare by Germany might be met with a limited response rather than commitment to general war. Clearly the United States was initiating measures to prepare for war, not implementing existing plans and policies. President Wilson and Secretary Baker knew full well that volunteering of the sort used to deal with the emergencies of the 19th century would not suffice in France. When the United States severed diplomatic relations with Germany in February, the president quietly told Baker to prepare a conscription bill for Congress. The resulting Selective Service Act of May 18, 1917, recommended volunteering to raise a million men for the duration of the war, but authorized conscription to accomplish it if there were shortfalls in recruiting.

President Woodrow Wilson photographed in the East Room of the White House on June 3, 1918, by Lt. E. DeBerri of the Signal Corps. (US Signal Corps, 12078)

Secretary of War Newton D. Baker with members of his inspection party and members of the AEF staff at the Hotel Crillon, Paris, in April 1918. Front row, left to right, General Pershing, Secretary Baker, US Ambassador to France William G. Sharp, and Major General William M. Black, chief of engineers. (US Signal Corps, 7555)

Major General Hugh L. Scott, chief-of-staff, United States Army, November 16, 1916, to September 21, 1917. General Scott accompanied former Secretary of War Elihu Root on an inspection tour of Russia in 1917. This photo was taken at Camp Dix, New Jersey, when Scott commanded the post in 1918. (US Signal Corps, 84778)

When Major General Hugh Scott, the chief-of-staff of the army from November 16, 1914, to September 21, 1917, notified General Pershing on May 2, 1917, that he was to organize four regiments of infantry and one of artillery from forces that he had commanded in the Southwest, he added that "if plans are carried out, you will be in command of the entire force." Pershing took that to mean a provisional division; the War Department meant the entire expeditionary army! There was only a rudimentary set of organizational documents and the effort was largely personal and ad hoc. On May 26 Secretary Baker forwarded Pershing a note containing the following instructions:

1. The President designates you to command all the land forces of the United States operating in Continental Europe and in the United Kingdom of Great Britain and Ireland, including any part of the Marine Corps which may be detached for service there with the Army. From your command are excepted the Military Attachés and others of the Army who may be on duty directly with our several embassies.

In addition to the usual administrative instructions, Pershing was to cooperate with the other countries operating against the Germans, with the "underlying idea" that the US forces "are a separate and distinct component of the combined forces, the identity of which must be preserved."

Clearly, General Pershing was to organize, train, and employ his forces in the general effort to defeat the Central Powers. Exactly how he was to do that was left up to him. Pershing judged that his instructions were "both admirable examples of the powers that should be invested in a commander in the field and were never changed or amplified in any essential."

Preparation for war

Every aspect of preparation was uphill for the AEF following the declaration of war. Rudimentary planning had been underway at the War Department since Pershing's punitive expedition was operating in the Southwest and Mexico in 1916, but no decisions regarding how the expeditionary field army was to be organized and equipped, nor about the tactical doctrine that was to govern its employment, had been taken. The AEF would be built stone by stone based on the experience of a few general staff officers, the accumulated "lessons" of earlier field operations of the US Army and Navy in the war with Spain, and the advice of military missions from France and Great Britain. Additionally, a US military mission headed by Colonel Chauncey B. Baker, Quartermaster Corps, traveled to Belgium, France, and Great Britain in June and July 1917 to visit "training camps and other military establishments, both in the zone of the interior and the zone of operations." It is hard to avoid the image of an ad hoc process of mobilization, training, and deployment of an American field army to France, but the few professionals who had experienced earlier mobilizations were making reasonable efforts in 1917.

It is a commonplace, however, that the United States was dramatically unprepared for entry into a major land war against European nations hardened by two-and-a-half years of grinding trench warfare. In notes prepared after the war, Brigadier General Fox Conner, the G-3 (operations officer) of the AEF, observed that on the threshold of US entry into the war German morale was high and an air of defeatism haunted the French. The Italians, as well as the Russians, might very well have been forced out of the war in 1917. Both England and France had spent their "best blood" and had their backs to the wall. "Black, indeed, were the Allied prospects—except for America!" General Pershing had noted in his final report to the Secretary of War in 1919, that "Prior to our entrance into the war, the regiments of our small army were very much scattered, and we had no organized units, even approximating a division, that could be sent overseas prepared to take the field." The preparedness movement had by the fall of 1915, "become a popular fad and a craze, riding the progressive currents of national efficiency and individual duty." But the preparedness movement was not to "get the United States ready to intervene in World War I;" rather it "was almost purely defensive. Its thrust was isolationist, not interventionist." It began as an effort by Leonard Wood and like-minded colleagues to reform the army and by the end of 1916 had "evolved into a drive for a universal military training which had previously been unthinkable," But, without doubt, the crusade that America launched across the Atlantic in the summer of 1917 was inchoate, a patchwork quilt of enthusiastic raw-boned youths, untrained but strong in numbers.

Pershing arrived in London with a small staff on June 9, 1917, and in France on June 13. The 1st Expeditionary Division was created from existing infantry, artillery, and engineer regiments and shipped to France, where their organization and training would take place near the field of battle. The 1st Division was Pershing's point of the spear and the base upon which he would build his army. He believed he would need a force of about one million men in order to achieve a "complete, well-balanced, and independent fighting organization"

General Pershing (left) and General Tom Bridges, British Army, inspecting the Guard of Honor upon Pershing's arrival at Liverpool, England, in June 1917. Bridges was a member of the British Mission to the United States. (US Signal Corps, 95567)

to conduct offensive operations in 1918; the future, he noted, might require three times that number. It is clear that the new commander-in-chief understood that there was more to effective employment of his AEF than doctrine and training. He also needed, amongst other things, motivated officers at all levels, an experienced GHQ staff, and a functioning logistic system. Major General Hanson Ely, whose 28th Infantry Regiment made the successful attack on Cantigny, noted, "Many of our soldiers had received but little training before going into battle, a fact which swelled our casualties. Most of them were still, in a large measure, untrained when the war ended."

Pershing believed that American doctrine, that is the standard procedure for how American combat units would train and fight, should be based on the principle that "the rifle and the bayonet remain the supreme weapons of the infantry soldier and that the ultimate success of the army depends on their proper use in open warfare." The "how we should fight" doctrine was published in two key documents: *Infantry Drill Regulations, 1911* and *Field Service Regulations, 1914*. The *Infantry Drill Regulations* explained how infantry units from platoon to brigade should train and fight, while the *Field Service Regulations* provided similar guidance for divisions and larger units. Both manuals were revised several times to keep pace with organizational changes and the tactical lessons from battlefield experience.

Based on his own observations, and those of his staff, of the French and British, Pershing knew that he needed to establish a formal system of training schools to impart this basic concept to newly inducted officers, noncommissioned officers, and soldiers. The training was to be based on the experience of the 1st Division in a progressive, three-stage program. The exigencies of the war, however, were to thwart this orderly plan. The 1st Division barely completed the program and none of the following divisions came close to being fully prepared for battle.

Secretary of War Baker and his War Department General Staff of 19 officers faced an enormous task in April 1917. The February 14, 1903, act of Congress created the general staff but did not cancel the very powerful service department bureaus. The nation, with its robust manufacturing capabilities, had been supporting Britain and France but at the expense of building up the American armed forces. When Baker took over from acting Secretary of War Major General Hugh Scott on March 9, 1916, there was no plan to send American forces to France. President Wilson had been angry when he learned in the fall of 1915 that the general staff had been doing some contingency planning for a war with Germany, but he clearly misunderstood the nature of that speculative thinking by his military professionals. Prior to the declaration of war in April 1917, the president was consistently looking for ways to avoid American involvement in the European war.

Given the unsettled nature of political and diplomatic activity in the months prior to April 1917, it is not surprising that the army did little to prepare for overseas service. Wilson was acutely aware of the preparedness advocates and the domestic political danger posed by their criticism. The officer training camps established at Plattsburg, New York, and several other places were initiatives of these political adversaries. There was no formal training structure for a large mass army in existence at the point of American entry into the war. It all had to be created at the same time as the first contingent—the 1st Expeditionary Division—was pulled together from the Texas–Mexico border area and literally assembled aboard ship on the east coast. The 2d Division was formed by adding to units already organized and in transit to France. The 5th Marine Regiment was attached to the 1st Division for movement, but attached to the 4th Brigade, 2d Division, in France. The 3d Infantry Brigade, with the 9th and 23d Infantry Regiments, was also moving toward the theater of war. What remained was to gather up the units to make up the 4th Infantry Brigade at Gettysburg, Pennsylvania, but the War and Navy Departments decided to form a Marine Brigade instead. The 2d Division headquarters opened

Brigadier General Paul B. Malone. "Follow Me" Malone was the initial AEF training chief. He later commanded a regiment and a brigade in the 5th Division. (US Signal Corps, 40143)

at Bourmont in the Department of Haute Marne on October 26, 1917. Brigadier General Charles A. Doyen, USMC, assumed temporary command until Major General Omar Bundy, US Army, relieved him on November 8. And so it went as units were knitted together into fighting divisions.

Private Herbert L. McHenry, later assigned as a machine gunner in the 16th Infantry Regiment, recalled his arrival for basic training at Camp Lee, Virginia, on May 29, 1918. Sixty-two percent of the inductees in McHenry's cohort were rejected for physical reasons. The new soldiers received their Enfield rifles after about ten days of drill and other processing activities. McHenry and his fellow soldiers destined for France left Camp Lee on July 17 and marched to City Point, Virginia, to board a river boat for Newport News where they boarded the *Czaritza*, an old Russian passenger ship. The 5,000 soldiers arrived at Brest, France, on July 29. After a ride in a "Forty and Eight" boxcar to Tours, the logistical headquarters of the AEF, McHenry traded his Enfield for a Springfield rifle and received some bayonet drill. After several more days of marching and train riding, the new 1st Division men reached their destination. It was probably that way for most of the American boys joining the AEF.

Training in the US

Lieutenant Joseph Dorst Patch was in the 26th Infantry Regiment stationed at Texas City, then a part of the 2d Division commanded by Major General J. Franklin Bell. He remembered that training consisted of "marksmanship (rifle and pistol), drill (close and extended order) and long hard marches in heavy marching order." Patch's battalion sailed on the *Momus*, late of the United Fruit Line, on June 14, where the machine gunners were issued the troublesome Benét-Mercié machine guns, "complicated pieces of air-cooled mechanisms, which almost required a jeweler to strip and assemble." The troops had never seen or fired those guns and fortunately received "better guns overseas."

While the units of the Regular Army and the National Guard in federal service were available within the four continental departments, Hawaii and the Philippines, the total of 9,693 officers and 203,864 enlisted men would provide only seven divisions if every soldier was mobilized for overseas service. The Selective Service system brought more than 2.8 million men to the training camps during America's period of belligerency, most co-located with army posts. Additional housing had to be constructed at the existing camps and an additional 32 camps—16 each for the National Guard and the Regular Army—were built. Many of the new camps were built in the South or the Southeast, mostly because of the favorable weather and training conditions. Each camp was designed for about 40,000 trainees, but General Pershing's reorganization proposal of July 10, 1918, raised the strength of infantry companies from 150 to 250 soldiers, and so the barracks were too small! But it was not the barracks problem that slowed the commencement of training until September 1917. The culprits were the slow and somewhat cumbersome induction process and the shortages of equipment and supplies. Nonetheless, the temporary camps sufficed to gain the necessary momentum to raise, equip, and train the initial troop cohorts of the army.

The acquisition and training of officers was a bit more complicated. The National Defense Act of 1916 made provisions for reserve forces for the regular establishment and the National Guard. However, the nation never came close to recruiting those numbers that were authorized. On the day that the United States entered World War I, 5,960 officers were present for duty; but this was 1,292 officers short of authorized strength. Moreover, reports from France showed that attrition within the infantry units required additional manpower above authorized strength to absorb what the British called "wastage." Ultimately General Pershing decided to designate a handful of arriving divisions in France as support or "depot" divisions. The 41st Division fulfilled this role in General Hunter Liggett's I Corps, mostly because Colonel

Brigadier General Harold B. Fiske followed Malone as AEF training chief. Fiske was responsible for developing and implementing the AEF training program in France. (US Signal Corps, 24359)

Douglas MacArthur, the chief-of-staff of the newly arrived 42d Division (Rainbow), argued strenuously that his division should not be parceled out as replacements for other divisions. At the Armistice on November 11, 1918, there were 203,786 officers in a total force of 3,685,458 or about 5.5 percent.

The first 16 training camps for officers opened on May 15, 1917, patterned on the Plattsburg model. Plattsburg Barracks (NY), Fort Benjamin Harrison (IN), and Fort Sheridan (IL) each hosted two camps, and ten other army posts each supported one camp. The first training cycle ended on August 11, with 27,341 men commissioned. Three more cycles, the last ending in February 1919, produced more officers while training was first decentralized to divisions, then re-centralized to take the burden off deploying divisions. A training camp for African-American officers was in operation at Fort Des Moines (IA) from June 18 to October 18, 1918, resulting in 639 commissioned officers from an admitted group of 1,250 candidates. Several other special officer-training camps were conducted in 1918. The total number of officers commissioned from all camps was 80,568, with 48,968 of those in the infantry and 20,291 in the artillery.

In order to sustain divisions that had mobilized and were beginning to deploy in the last half of 1917, the United States accepted the offers of France and Britain to supply officers and noncommissioned officers to train American soldiers in the US camps.

In September 1917, the Third Bureau of the French General Staff commented on the substance of the training program and noted that it showed only a battalion sector and greatly simplified the complex tasks of organizing the position of an infantry division for trench warfare. The relationship between realistic training and actual combat was emphasized by the idea that in organizing positions "Bloody losses [will be] sustained by ignorance, error, or laziness."

Although this dependence on foreign trainers relieved the strain on deploying divisions and those already in France who did not have to supply stay-behind detachments of officers and noncommissioned officers, the French and British trainers had their own agenda. Instead of adhering to the US doctrine based on open warfare and rifle marksmanship, the training program was based on fighting from trenches. The two foreign missions persuaded the US War Department that the approach was sound, which immediately put the program in the United States in conflict with General Pershing's three-phase training program in France. In reality, French instructors steeped in the doctrine of trench warfare also dominated the program in France. Pershing did realize that he must depend on the host trainers, at least in the early stages of preparing soldiers and units up to battalion strength, to toughen the troops to the rigors of warfare on the Western Front.

Training in France

The 1st Division led the first group of American divisions into the theater of war. As the troop units were arriving, the AEF staff began operations in Paris before moving to the new General Headquarters (GHQ) at Chaumont on September 1, 1917. It comprised 1,342 officers, clerks, and enlisted men. The training section had been added to the staff on August 11. Lieutenant Colonel Paul B. Malone headed the AEF training section (G-5). When he was transferred to the 3d Division in February 1918 to command a brigade, his assistant, Colonel Harold B. Fiske, who remained the chief AEF trainer until the end of the war, replaced him. Malone and Fiske shaped the AEF training and education programs. Like all the primary staff, Pershing handpicked them.

Clustered in French villages around Chaumont, the arriving divisions, less their artillery brigades, which were sent to Valdahon in the southeast of France, took up the routine of training their soldiers and their units up through battalions.

The 1st Division established the training pattern. Harold Fiske had begun his service in the 16th Infantry Regiment shortly before it arrived in France with the 1st Division. He recalled in a memo adter the war that:

A large part of the company officers had been recently … commissioned; many had only just finished the three months course at [Fort] Leavenworth.

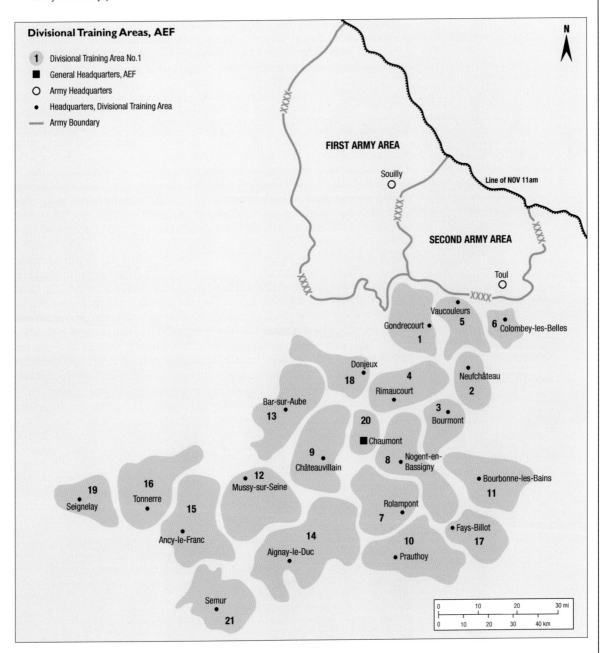

Divisional Training Areas, AEF

1 Divisional Training Area No.1
■ General Headquarters, AEF
O Army Headquarters
• Headquarters, Divisional Training Area
— Army Boundary

N

FIRST ARMY AREA

Souilly

Line of NOV 11am

SECOND ARMY AREA

Toul

Vaucouleurs
Gondrecourt •   5   6 • Colombey-les-Belles
1

Donjeux
18   4   Neufchâteau
Rimaucourt   2

Bar-sur-Aube
13   20   3 • Bourmont

■ Chaumont

9   8 • Nogent-en-
Châteauvillain   Bassigny

• 12   • Bourbonne-les-Bains
Mussy-sur-Seine   11

19   16
Seignelay Tonnerre   15   Rolampont
7

14   10   • Fays-Billot
Ancy-le-Franc   Aignay-le-Duc   17
• Prauthoy

Semur
21

0   10   20   30 mi
0   10   20   30   40 km

This map depicts the divisional training areas assigned to the AEF in northeastern France. Also shown are the areas of operation for First Army (organized August 10, 1918) and Second Army (organized October 10, 1918) and the Armistice line of November 11, 1918. AEF GHQ is shown in area 20 at Chaumont. The 1st Division HQ is in area 1 at Gondrecourt, the 2d Division HQ is in area 9 at Châteauvillain and the 42d Division was assigned to the 5th training area at Vaucouleurs. Not all numbers coincide with divisions of the same numbers. The 21 training areas were principally infantry training areas. The field artillery trained at Le Valdahon to the southeast near the Swiss border.

A thousand recruits had been received a day or two before my arrival, and others were continually arriving in the effort of the War Department to bring the regiment to its new strength. None of these recruits seemed to have had any instruction ... No machine guns were at hand ... The Infantry of the 1st Division sailed for France about June 12th. As usual no arrangements for overstrength [that is, to include first replacements] had been made; so that each company sailed from six to 15 men short of its complement. I think the experience of the 16th Infantry can be taken as in every way like that of each of the other infantry regiments. The 1st Division received no training in the United States. Its time in the United States was one of reorganization, re-armament, change and confusion.

A memorandum governing divisional training was issued by Fiske's office on July 18, 1917. It described "fundamental principles" of training for the 1st Division and other divisions that were to follow into the theater of operations. It confirmed that the principles of "discipline, command and combat" set forth in the *Drill, Small Arms* and *Field Service* regulations "remain unchanged," that is rifle marksmanship and open warfare remained at the core of training guidance for American divisions. It also confirmed that offensive, not defensive (meaning trench) warfare was "the basis of instruction." Three months would be devoted to "Preliminary" training, that is individual and small unit training. This would be followed by one month of "Divisional" training that emphasized "the perfection of team work in actual fighting." Thus, Pershing and his training staff believed that American divisions could be readied for effective combat operations in four months.

The (Colonel Chauncey) Baker board reported its findings on July 11, 1917. One of the recommendations stated "That the United States make no essential change in its system of physical training, close order and disciplinary drills and musketry." Closely associated with the progressive training of divisions as they arrived in France was the establishment of professional schools, both for the AEF at large, but also within corps and divisions to continue the education of officers and noncommissioned officers. It is clear that Pershing anticipated that he would need to replace the French and British trainers, both in France and in the camps in the United States, as soon as practicable so that the Americans

Lieutenant Colonel George S. Patton, Jr., commander of the American tank training school and center at Bourg, France. He is standing in front of a Renault light tank. (US Signal Corps, 17592)

could take charge of their own training and impart the "American style" of combat rather than the defensive, trench warfare doctrine favored by the French and to, a degree, by the British.

Schools in France

Training schools, both at the level of the AEF and within divisions and corps, were essential to disseminate doctrine and to raise the skill levels of officers and noncommissioned officers. General Pershing pulled Brigadier General Robert L. Bullard from command of the 2d Brigade of the 1st Division in July 1917 and assigned him as commanding general, AEF schools. Bullard's task was to train infantry officers for combat. Pershing was well acquainted with Bullard's capabilities as a trainer, having known him at West Point and in Texas before the war. His confidence was not misplaced and by November Bullard had his infantry school staffed and operating. The bugaboo that plagued the AEF schools was the necessity to detach officers from line divisions to attend as students and to serve as faculty—all at the expense of the fighting power of the line divisions. It was a left pocket, right pocket decision as to where experienced officers and noncommissioned officers were needed most. This was one of the several most important choices that Pershing made in organizing, training, and fighting his AEF in France.

American officers, officer candidates, and noncommissioned officers were sent to existing British and French schools as the Americans brought their own facilities up to speed. In addition to AEF level schools, Fiske anticipated that schooling would have to occur at army, corps, and division levels in order to sustain the movement of experienced personnel into the combat divisions, the tip of the fighting machine. During the transition from British/French schools to AEF schools, the Americans depended upon the British for expert instruction in the Stokes mortar, sniping, scouting, use of the bayonet, and musketry (marksmanship). The French instructors tutored their American pupils in tactics, grenades, automatic rifles, 37mm guns, machine guns, and field fortifications. The courses varied from two to seven weeks in length. While the schools were centralized to make the best use of meager resources, training was based on the division. The critically important relationship between educated leaders and the combat effectiveness of the divisions was proved in the fighting of the spring and fall of 1918. The center for AEF schools was established at Langres, an old fortress town with plentiful barracks situated 22 miles southeast of the AEF headquarters at Chaumont; Colonel James A. McAndrew was appointed commandant on October 10, 1917, and Brigadier General Alfred W. Bjornstad served as the first director of the staff college. Forty-two officers, of a class of 75, graduated from the first three-month course and were qualified for staff duty with divisions and corps. A full array of schools, patterned on the school system in the United States, came into operation in the fall of 1917. Artillery, aviation, military police, engineering, machine gunnery, intelligence, gas operations, and even musicians and dentists had their own schools. Fiske intended to have the various corps headquarters supervise their own schools, but soon discovered that those organizations were on the move too frequently. He placed the corps schools under AEF control. Most of the instruction at the corps schools was of four weeks' duration. In May 1918, the aviation sections of the corps schools were consolidated in the II Corps area.

As noted earlier, the only division to complete its intended four-month training cycle was the 1st Division. General Pershing relied heavily on the training of the 1st Division to set the framework for the training of all AEF divisions as they arrived in France. On October 4, 1917, he wrote to Secretary Baker and reported "A tentative system of instruction and training has been outlined, based upon the best information obtainable, and schools of instruction have been organized to provide instructors. The French have helped us train the 1st Division, while the British are taking as many young officers as they can accommodate in their schools." He continued to explain his ideas of offensive warfare and his policy of rejecting senior officers who were physically unfit or not in accord with his philosophy of command in combat. He closed by asking the support of the War Department in recognizing his officers with promotions. The commander-in-chief was pleased with the progress of the 1st Division and judged it to be efficient and "later to become famous among the armies on the Western Front."

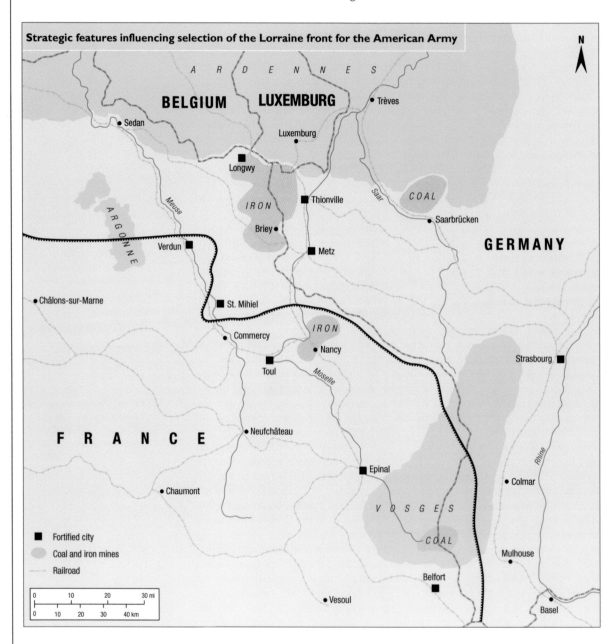

Strategic features influencing selection of the Lorraine front for the American Army

N

ARDENNES

BELGIUM   LUXEMBURG   • Trèves

• Sedan   Luxemburg •

■ Longwy

IRON   ■ Thionville   Saar   COAL
Briey •   • Saarbrücken

Meuse   GERMANY

ARGONNE

Verdun ■   ■ Metz

• Châlons-sur-Marne   ■ St. Mihiel   IRON
• Commercy   • Nancy   Strasbourg ■
Toul ■   Moselle

FRANCE   • Neufchâteau

• Chaumont   Epinal •   Rhine
• Colmar

VOSGES

■ Fortified city   COAL   Mulhouse •
Coal and iron mines   Belfort ■
Railroad   • Vesoul   Basel

| 0 | 10 | 20 | 30 mi |
| 0 | 10 | 20 | 30 | 40 km |

This map shows some of the strategic considerations for locating the AEF in northeastern France. As a late arrival to the theater of operations the AEF had to be accommodated in an area where it would not interfere with the operations of the British in the north and French in the center of the Western Front. There had to be adequate training space to receive, organize and train the Americans in a relatively quiet sector. The northeast was a terminus for the AEF line of communication from the arrival ports in western France and south of Paris. The rail lines closer to the front were all fully occupied. The countryside could provide food and draft animals to support the training.

Major General William L. Sibert, who had deployed the 1st Division to France, commanded them during this period of intensive training. As was to be expected, General Pershing closely observed the division's progress and occasionally provided corrections. Lieutenant Colonel George C. Marshall, the division operations officer, recounted that "Like an only child, we suffered from too much attention, and found ourselves often irritated by the frequent visits of investigators, inspectors and others from the higher command." During the period of training in early September 1917 near Gondrecourt, Georges Clemenceau, soon to be Premier of France, visited the 1st Division. After watching a boxing match at the 26th Infantry Regiment's Field Day, he was impressed by the offensive spirit and "rugged fighting qualities" displayed by the regiment. Clemenceau, unable to meet with General Pershing, returned with General Noel Marie Joseph Edward de Curières de Castelnau, his chief-of-staff, to discuss the entry of the 1st Division into the line in a quiet sector in about ten days. Sibert demurred and explained that only General Pershing could make that decision. Clemenceau, speaking in English, argued that the time for action was at hand. The French army, he said, "was exhausted" and it was imperative that training schedules must be subordinated to the overall needs of the war. General Sibert, according to Marshall, tactfully but forcefully explained that to commit the 1st Division before it was properly trained "would be taking a very grave risk, the unfortunate results of which would react as heavily against the French and English" as against the Americans. The 1st Division, assumed by many to be the "pick of the Regular Army," was in fact "an entirely new organization and its ranks were filled with recruits." To risk a defeat would "have a calamitous effect on the morale of the American soldier and on the Allies as well."

The 1st Division, nonetheless, moved ahead with its training and in mid-October was occupying positions on the Lorraine front between Lunéville and Nancy. This sector of rolling countryside had been quiet since 1915. The first battalions of the four infantry regiments of the division (16, 18, 26, 28),

School of Aviation at Vineuil, 1917, by Henri Farré. There are two villages in France that bear the name Vineul that could have been the site of Farré's painting. The first is near the classification center for the AEF at Blois (where failed commanders were sent). The more likely location, however, is 28km west and slightly south of the major AEF flying field at Issoudun, near Chateauroux. Farré was a well-know painter of aviation scenes. (1st Division Museum)

each with a machine-gun company, and detachments of engineers and signal troops, joined the 18th French Infantry Division in the line. One battalion each from the three artillery regiments of the division left their training site at Valdahon and joined their fellow doughboys during the night of October 22. The next morning, C Battery, 6th Field Artillery fired "the first shot from an American-manned gun." During the night of November 2–3, the Germans conducted a trench raid on the positions of F Company, 16th Infantry, and within minutes three doughboys were lying dead in the trench bottom and 11 others were being marched into captivity. Training was evolving into combat.

Although combining the general staff functions of operations and training into a single section supervised by one chief would help ensure that troops would be trained "in accordance with the same doctrine to be used in fighting them," General Pershing decided to establish the two functions into separate staff sections because of span of control and the primacy of both functions for success in combat. General Fiske initially thought separate sections were a bad idea, but as the AEF staff developed he saw the wisdom of his chief's decision. In order to train continually while battle raged, the AEF needed an overstrength of at least 50 percent in officers and men. A corps was determined to need six divisions, two of which would be depot or replacement divisions. One of these feeder divisions would be located immediately to the rear of the four combat divisions to "hold and train replacements in officers and men all the way from the division commander to the private soldier." The other division was located near the ports of entry into France to receive new men from the United States, give them some individual training to include marksmanship, then to pass these men forward to the replacement division in the zone of operations for the rest of their preparation. Ultimately the port-stationed division idea was abandoned in favor of larger troop administrative centers. The nature of the replacement process, Fiske pointed out, governed the entire school system for the AEF. As combat operations began in the spring of 1918, "our wastage in officers was enormous from the beginning and beyond all of our anticipations." But the demands of officers and noncommissioned officers for the schools and for service in the rapidly expanding logistics organization, the SOS, also produced "wastage" from the line divisions and from the available pool of new men arriving from the United States. Nearly 11,000 new officers emerged from the candidate schools in the various arms up to the time of the Armistice. In the United States, the classification system was shunting the very best officer prospects into the Air Service and the other specialty arms at the very time that infantry leaders were needed in the line divisions. "This combing of divisions robbed them of officer material and greatly delayed their preparation for battle."

Mobilization and training continued to propel the engine of the AEF from the rear. In France finding a way to accommodate French training methods and doctrine, finding enough French-speaking doughboys, and securing adequate billets and transport continually challenged the AEF staff. The winter of 1917–18 presented arduous training conditions, including inadequate cold weather clothing and equipment for the troops. After the war and the return of the AEF to the United States, Major General James W. McAndrew, former chief-of-staff of the AEF, wrote of the military lessons of the World War. He said that:

> If unprepared when war comes, it takes more than a year to call out, organize, equip, and train armies to meet the trained soldiery of our enemies ... We know that the training of the officers to organize, instruct, supply and lead our combat units in battle is a matter not of weeks or of months, but of years ... that higher leaders in war and the staff officers to whom must fall the hardest problems to solve, must be the products of a life-time study of their profession ... the fact remains that ... it was 14 months after our entry into the war before the American Army became a real factor in the struggle.

Command, control, communication, and intelligence

The raising and support of a field army and its effective battle employment are related, but quite different. The former is based on recruiting and personnel policies, tables of organization and equipment, and logistical organization. The latter is very much a matter of doctrine, training, and leadership. In this regard General Pershing's AEF in France and the War Department in Washington were often at odds about matters of command and control.

Secretary of War Newton D. Baker and his party viewing action at the front in March 1918. They used a railway flat car as an observation platform. (7776)

ABOVE Secretary of War Newton D. Baker and Private Carlisle Babcock, 2d Division, March 20, 1918, taken while Baker and General Pershing were making an inspection of the Lines of Communication. (US Signal Corps, 8453)

On March 6, 1917, President Woodrow Wilson selected the former mayor of Cleveland to succeed Lindley M. Garrison as secretary of war. Newton D. Baker was described by his biographer as "a slim little man with a fighting jaw

and a whimsical eye." Major General John Pershing called on the new secretary of war in Washington in May 1917. "I was surprised to find him much younger and considerably smaller than I had expected." The soon to be commander-in-chief of the AEF quickly changed his impression after Baker explained why he selected Pershing ahead of a number of more senior officers to command in France. "He was courteous and pleasant," recalled Pershing, "and impressed me as being frank, fair, and business-like." Still under the impression that he was to command a division, Pershing returned to Secretary Baker's office several days later and learned that he was to command the entire AEF.

LEFT Secretary of War Newton D. Baker with Major General James G. Harbord at HQ, Services of Supply, Tours, reviewing Quartermaster troops. (US Signal Corps, 23779)

Newton D. Baker was a strong supporter of War Department reform and of General Peyton C. March, the army's chief-of-staff. Baker was able to steer a course between the animosities and jealousies that sprouted in both the War Department General Staff and in the AEF General Staff. Moreover, President Wilson had confidence in his judgment and managerial skills. Not just an office warrior, Mr. Baker traveled to the theater of war in France twice. He arrived in September 1918 in time to view the attack against the St. Mihiel salient by the newly established American First Army. Accompanied by Count de Chambrun, related to Lafayette, Baker walked through the streets of the city that was the home of both the marquis and the president of France, Raymond Poincaré. According to his biographer, the diminutive secretary of war had a good look at America's army at war.

Newton D. Baker had replaced Lindley M. Garrison at the War Department helm on March 9, 1916, after a short caretaker period under the direction of Major General Hugh L. Scott, chief-of-staff of the army. Baker had wanted Major General Peyton C. March for army chief after Scott stepped down in September 1917 and Major General Tasker H. Bliss left for France and service with the Supreme War Council in May 1918. General Pershing instead sent his friend Major General John Biddle to Washington where the competing interests, both civilian and military, quickly overwhelmed him. March replaced him and arrived from France to take up his duties on May 19, 1918, giving Baker a younger, more vigorous leader of the army who set to making his new jurisdiction more efficient. It is important to note this civil–military arrangement because it lies at the heart of the American system of command and control of the armed forces. A major dispute as to who commanded the army—the civilian secretary or the senior uniformed officer—had been settled in 1903 with the passage of the General Staff legislation. The Overman Act (May 20, 1918) confirmed the president's authority to act in emergencies and solidified the primacy of the executive branch of the government in directing the nation's wartime efforts.

Command and control

Field command of the army in France was the exclusive responsibility of General Pershing, and Secretary Baker confirmed that on several occasions. Pershing exercised control of the army by careful selection of his subordinate commanders and staff officers. The evolution of the General Headquarters, AEF, at Chaumont solidified that control. But the challenges were larger and more numerous than merely creating a general headquarters and staff. There were corps and divisions, and eventually two field armies, which had to be organized and trained at the same time. Pershing relied again on trusted subordinates for this work, notably Major Generals James G. Harbord, Robert L. Bullard, James W. McAndrew, Hunter Liggett, Joseph T. Dickman, and Brigadier Generals Harold B. Fiske, Paul B. Malone and, importantly, Fox Conner. Pershing's style of command was direct, personal, and often intrusive. There was no question as to who the boss was and what he wanted in the way of performance and efficiency. Colonel George C. Marshall, during the darker days of the Meuse–Argonne campaign, noted that the commander-in-chief "carried himself with an air of relentless determination to push the operation to a decisive

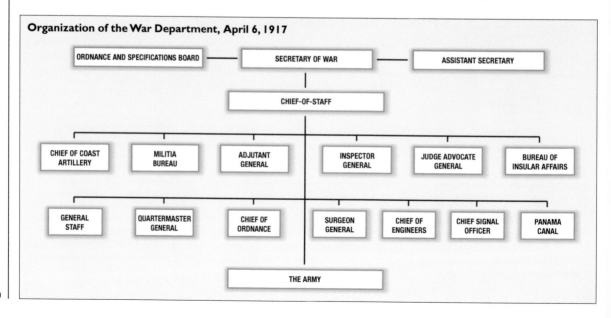

Organization of the War Department, April 6, 1917

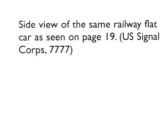

victory." His bearing and demeanor "inspired confidence" but made clear that he would truck no slacking or "weak-hearted" efforts. Major General Hunter Liggett, perhaps Pershing's favorite corps, and later army, commander said of his senior, "General Pershing had absolute authority, and his standards were drastic, to the great good fortune of the American Army." Regarding his abilities to work with those over whom he had no authority, Major General James G. Harbord, his most trusted chief-of-staff, said on the occasion of the Americans' visit to the Baker Board in London in early July 1917, "General Pershing showed much tact and patience" in dealing with a group of officers that had expressed disagreement with his views. He won them over and influenced their report to Washington regarding policies to govern the AEF.

Charles P. Summerall, who had been a member of the Baker Board, assumed command of the 1st Division on July 15, 1918, at the outset of the Soissons campaign to reduce the Marne salient. He was an extraordinary combat leader. Late in life he wrote an autobiographical "diary" of his military career. Speaking of the challenges to leadership in the Soissons campaign, he commented on the stress of combat:

> At another time, the division was to attack by orders of the French Corps at 4:30pm. At 4:25pm the colonel of a regiment called me and

ABOVE General Tasker H. Bliss visiting II Corp HQ at Fruges, July 19, 1918. (US Signal Corps, 17226)

General Tasker Howard Bliss was viewed as a competitor by Pershing, but the former army chief-of-staff was the ideal choice to represent the United States on the Supreme War Council formed at the Rapallo Conference in November 1917. Bliss had been acting chief-of-staff of the army while General Hugh Scott accompanied the Root Mission to Russia in 1917. Like Pershing and March, Bliss had been a military attaché. His service in Madrid during the Spanish–American war was uneventful, mostly because of the secretive behavior of his hosts and the short period of hostilities, but Bliss learned the ways of the diplomat that were to serve him well in France. Bliss enjoyed the confidence of both Secretary of War Newton Baker and presidential envoy

"Colonel" Edward House, the political representative of the United States at the Supreme War Council. When General Pershing found himself at odds with the other senior commanders in France over issues that were part military and part political, such as the amalgamation controversy, it was General Bliss who provided the iron hand in the velvet glove at the Supreme War Council to preserve his field commander's prerogatives and independence of action. Pershing respected Bliss and welcomed his support during difficult times. Bliss occasionally was frustrated by Pershing's high-handed behavior with his peers but believed that the commander-in-chief must be supported. It was a good partnership.

General Pershing with Marshal Henri Pétain, commander of the French Army and hero of the epic fighting at Verdun in 1916, at Chaumont, January 14, 1919. (US Signal Corps, 39676)

said that he could not obey the order and would not attack. I told him as calmly as possible that he must not say anything to his battalion commanders whom I knew would attack. He showed himself unsuited to be a combat regimental commander. The battalion commanders led their troops to take their objectives. I found that the colonel's connections were such that it would be best not to relieve him, but after the battle he was transferred out of the division. Thus, the two colonels in a brigade stated they could not obey an attack order and the brigade commander was too worn and mentally confused to force the attack. Such was the terrible ordeal of battle on officers.

General Summerall's philosophy of combat leadership was direct and to the point. Instead of punishing officers and soldiers for cowardice, he dealt with what he called "cases of neurosis" by appealing to the shirker's sense of duty. "The great mass of officers and men will overcome their fears and the further they are to the front the less they fear." When the "Division Judge" presented him with charges for cowardice, Summerall said "I told him to destroy the charges and send the men to their colonels who would at once place them in the front lines where their fears would disappear or the other men would take care of them. The difficulty disappeared as the men had more experience in battle." General Summerall believed that failure in combat is attributable more to "a state of mind of officers and men which deprives them of a desire to fight" than to "the resistance of the enemy." Leaders must "by personal contact and assurance inculcate and maintain a will to win in every member of his command," he said. "I never tried a man for cowardice." Later in the war, General Summerall's own judgment was called into question when his vague orders to his beloved 1st Division, then commanded by Brigadier General Frank Parker, to seize Sedan caused a near disaster as the 1st marched across the fronts of the 77th and 42d Divisions, "capturing" Brigadier General Douglas MacArthur and several of his officers. As it turned out, Summerall's understanding of the mission from General Pershing, and the desire of both to have the Americans in at the finish, led to the problem. George Marshall recalled that the First Army's chief-of-staff, Brigadier General Hugh Drum, approved the draft prepared by Marshall to carry out the commander-in-chief's desire that the First Army be the first Allied troops to enter Sedan. Drum inserted the controversial sentence "Boundaries will not be considered binding." Hunter Liggett said of Parker's handling of the mission that he "marched the division in seven columns—handling 25,000 men like a battalion—right through the First Army Corps upon Sedan." Pershing, perhaps recognizing his own mistake, shrugged the incident off, but Generals Dickman, then commanding I Corps, and Summerall, V Corps commander, carried the grudge well into the postwar years.

Officers of the G-2 (intelligence) section of the 5th Division general staff studying the battle maps in the Bois de Tuilerie near Montfaucon during the Meuse–Argonne campaign. (US Signal Corps, 28314)

ABOVE General (4-star) Peyton Conway March, chief-of-staff, US Army. (US Signal Corps, 31190)

Peyton Conway March, Lafayette College class of 1884 and West Point class of 1888, was in many respects similar to John J. Pershing—a "grim countenance,"

straight military bearing and a "strict disciplinarian but a fair one."

An artillery officer, Major March served in the Philippines as aide-de-camp to Major General Arthur MacArthur and on the First Army general staff in that theater. Brigadier General March deployed to France in June 1917 in command of the artillery brigade of the 42d Division, was promoted to major general, and, later in November, was assigned to command the AEF artillery at Valdahon. In February 1918, Major General March was selected by Secretary of War Newton D. Baker to become chief-of-staff of the army. His promotion to four-star rank in May 1918 placed him, along with former army

chief, General Tasker H. Bliss, in that small group of officers of equivalent rank and often competing objectives. In Washington, Baker and March overhauled the creaking War Department administration and endeavored to improve its efficiency. Realignment of the general staff along functional lines supplanted many traditional bureau responsibilities and created the Chemical Warfare Service, the Air Service, the Tank Corps, and several supply branches. He abolished the three categories of Regular Army, National Guard, and National Army in favor of a single unified army. John Pershing believed that March was dismantling army traditions.

LEFT Major General Joseph T. Dickman with Brigadier General Malin Craig and Colonel A.C. Voris, October 23, 1918. (US Signal Corps, 28332)

Major General Joseph T. Dickman commanded consecutively the 3d Division, IV Corps and, after the Armsitice, Third Army. He was one of the most effective officers in the AEF. A West Point graduate, class of 1881, he began his career in the cavalry with service on the western frontier and in army schools until 1898. In the Spanish–American war he served on Major General Joe Wheeler's staff in Cuba, then in the Philippines commanding an infantry

regiment. More schooling and service with the War Department General Staff prepared him for his appointment to the rank of general officer in 1917. He took command of the regular 3d Division and deployed with them to France in April and May 1918. In early June General Dickman deployed his division south of the Marne River near Château-Thierry and blunted the German drive in the Aisne–Marne salient. The 3d Division earned its nickname, "Rock of the Marne," during that operation. On October 12, Dickman took over command of I Corps from Major General Hunter Liggett, and, on November 15, he was promoted to command Third Army.

The point is that in high command, personality and style always matter. Virtually all of the senior commanders of the AEF were graduates of the relevant army schools and knew each other reasonably well. As Timothy Nenninger pointed out, however, it was not so much the commanders themselves, but rather "the process of command" that had been learned and codified in the AEF that mattered. Here was a major vulnerability of the expanding AEF—it was untested up until the serious fighting in the Aisne–Marne salient in July and August 1918. This is probably explained by the rapid mobilization, organization, training, and employment of the American combat and logistical units up to that point.

Communication

Critical to command of the army and its units in combat was control from top to bottom and reporting from bottom to top. Again, the fledgling American field army was learning what worked and what did not in the school of trial and error. At the company and battalion levels, where the action changed rapidly on the battlefield, control often depended on the strength

Sergeant W. B. Prince of the G-2 (intelligence) topographical section plotting the front lines of the 5th Division between Cuisy and Montfaucon during the Meuse–Argonne fighting. (US Signal Corps, 28295)

Field Signal Battalion

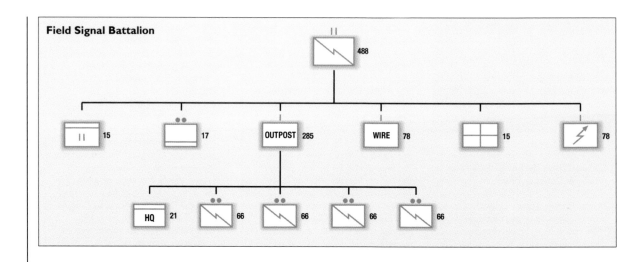

AEF Field Signal Battalions (Based on TO&E of June 26, 1918)

Personnel		
Unit/Section	**26 Jun '18**	**Strength**
Battalion HQ	1	15
Supply Section	1	17
Radio Company	1	78
Wire Company	1	78
Outpost Company	1	285
Total Combatants	–	**473**
Medical Dept.	–	15
Battalion Aggregate	1	**488**
Outpost Company Headquarters	1	21
Outpost Company Section	4	66 ea
Company Aggregate	–	285
Animals		
Draft Horses	–	12
Riding Horses	–	14 [incl. 5 with Outpost Co.]
Total Horses	–	**26**
Major Equipment Items		
Escort Wagons (2-horse)	–	4 [incl. 1 with Outpost Co.]
Water Carts	–	2
Reel Carts (2-horse)	–	6
Ration Carts	–	2
Rolling Kitchens	–	2
Combat Trucks (1½-ton, 4-wheel drive)	–	5 [incl. 1 with Outpost Co.]
Supply Trucks (1½-ton, 4-wheel drive)	–	5
Motor Cars	–	1

 (continued on page 25)

Motorcycles with Sidecar	–	15 [incl. 2 with Medical Detach. & 5 with Outpost Co.]
Motorcycles without Sidecar	–	6 [incl. I with Outpost Co.]
Pistols	–	473 [incl. 285 with Outpost Co.]

Source: United States Army In The World War 1917–1919. Volume 1: Organization of the American Expeditionary Forces (Washington: Historical Division, Department of the Army, 1948)

of character and intuitive ability of the junior officers and noncommissioned officers. Orders prior to battle were routinely communicated in writing by the five-paragraph field order learned in the army schools and detailed in the army's few manuals. Often time intervened, or the enemy did, and written orders were overtaken by verbal instructions from battalion to company commanders in person. There were no effective, reliable tactical radios, but there was wire and lots of it. Wire worked well in defensive positions, but not in the attack. Moving forward amidst the din of artillery, machine-gun, and mortar fire meant that platoon and company leaders had to rely on hand and arm signals, and runners. On the modern battlefield that technique could soon collapse, and did. For example, the operations officer of the AEF, Brigadier General Fox Conner, reported at the end of the war that as a result of the 1st Division's operations in the Soissons counteroffensive of July 1918, 60 percent of the division's infantry officers were killed or wounded. This sort of disruption to the chain of command had a far-reaching effect on the capability of infantry units to receive and execute combat orders simply because of the loss of experienced personnel. Training does not compensate for that sort of trauma. Replacements, even when immediately available, require time to absorb the standard operating procedures of their new unit. In the meantime, the unit suffers degradation in combat effectiveness. Above the company and battalion, the commanders and staffs did their best to gather useful intelligence, formulate clear orders, and provide the necessary support to ensure success in battle. They frequently fell short of the mark due to inexperience and incomplete training. Communication depended on wire supplemented by pigeon couriers and visual signaling with flares, flags, and lights. George Marshall recounted in his memoirs that during the final phase of operations in the Meuse–Argonne, several of his captains and lieutenants in the First Army operations section of GHQ wanted a chance to see

Sergeant Swanker of the Signal Corps pigeon section holding the first bird to carry a message during an attack near Cornieville, France, May 2, 1918. (US Signal Corps, 12001)

Recruiting posters for the Signal Corps Pigeon Service. (US Signal Corps, 67598)

Soldier demonstrating the use of the field signal projector lamp, August 27, 1917. (US Signal Corps, 17258)

some action. Marshall dispatched four of them as liaison officers and had the chief signal officer instruct them on how to send messages by pigeon courier. Each had an orderly with six pigeons and instructions to send messages at 0700hrs and 0900hrs, 1200hrs, and 1500hrs on November 1, then again at 0900hrs and 1300hrs on November 2. As the battle unfolded, the stalwart pigeons winged their way to First Army GHQ at Souilly with status reports and sketches. Marshall was able to turn this information around to the corps and division HQ by airplane drop before the reports had made their way from the front lines coming from lower to higher HQ! During this last phase of the fighting, "battle communication between Army Headquarters and the corps and divisions was difficult to manage, due to the rapidity of the advance," said Marshall. It took motorcycle messengers four to five hours to make their way forward over congested, torn-up roads. Wire communications had been disrupted during the course of the battle and the signal corps troops could not replace poles and lines quickly enough.

Intelligence

Intelligence is the processed product of information analyzed by experienced staff officers and noncommissioned officers. Intelligence operations of the AEF were of two types. The first was tactical, or battlefield, intelligence. This was administered by gleaning information from the Allied headquarters by means of military attachés and liaison officers. It usually was detailed and perishable, meaning that its value decreased with time from the point of its collection. Collection from interrogations of prisoners of war and questioning of local inhabitants as ground was recovered from the enemy yielded the most useful information. Aerial photographs and Air Service observer reports added to the inventory of available information.

The second type of intelligence was that generated by the War Department's military intelligence staff and the G-2 section of the AEF staff. This type of information included technical intelligence obtained from analysis of captured German equipment, changes in the political and economic conditions in the theater of war, and analysis of changes in German strategic and operational effectiveness. This intelligence, while of use to the AEF planners, had no real immediate use to the combat divisions. Had the war lasted into 1919 the combination of this sort of intelligence and tactical intelligence collection would have had a complementary effect on combat operations.

Telegraph trailer at First Army headquarters, Souilly, France, being moved out of danger from incoming fire during the Meuse–Argonne campaign, October 30, 1918. (US Signal Corps, 28413)

Organization

The principal element in the American Expeditionary Forces was the division. Major General John Pershing noted that in May of 1917 "no such unit then existed in our Army." It was an infantry fighting unit made more potent with the addition of artillery, machine-gun, and other combat support units. The organization of the army as authorized by the National Defense Act of 1916 had been published in tables of organization and equipment (TO&E) on May 3, 1917, but no divisions had yet been organized. The War College Division of the War Department General Staff prepared a provisional organization for an expeditionary division for service in France, using the TO&E of May 3, 1917. After consultations with the French and British military missions that were in the United States shortly after America entered the war as an associated power, and discussions with Pershing, it was understood that the provisional organization would require modification once the division arrived in France.

Entrance to the GHQ, AEF, in Chaumont, France. Building B beyond the fence housed the staff offices. The GHQ was located in the regimental barracks at Caserne de Damrémont. (US Signal Corps, 86446)

Organizing, mobilizing, training, deploying, and fighting of each division would have to occur sequentially in a compressed timetable of events. The pressures to cut corners and field fighting organizations before they were ready would be enormous. To counter this, General Pershing and his AEF staff, which was also being organized and trained at the same time, developed a logical, phased program to receive combat divisions and their support units in France. At the same time, with the help of General Tasker H. Bliss, the US military representative on the Supreme War Council after November 1917, Pershing was arguing for a separate mission with a separate zone of action for his AEF.

The organization, mobilization, and deployment would be in the hands of the War Department General Staff in Washington, DC, but as was quickly discovered, precious little training was to occur before deployment.

The AEF General Headquarters and staff

The General Headquarters of the AEF began its work in Paris. From that location on June 21, 1917, Lieutenant Colonel John McAuley Palmer, the AEF operations officer, and three other officers left to conduct a reconnaissance in the east to look for a home for the American staff and arriving divisions. The 1st Division's arrival that same month required accelerated staff work so that the AEF did not fall prey to the French Army's intention of organizing and training it according to French doctrine. On September 1, 1917, General Pershing ordered his staff to Chaumont in the Haute-Marne region, 72km south of Bar-Le-Duc "to be within easy reach of American training areas." The area chosen for the AEF was in Lorraine in the northeastern part of France.

Chaumont is situated on the heights where the feudal regions of Lorraine, Burgundy, and Champagne meet. Napoleon began his campaign of 1814 from the city, and his conquerors met to sign the peace there before marching on to Paris. The Caserne de Damrémont, a French regimental barracks, became the nerve center of the AEF during the active hostilities and later until July 11, 1919, when the Americans began the deployment back to Paris and on to the United States. When Pershing saw the barracks he knew at once it was what he was looking for. His office was to be in the center of building "B."

General John J. Pershing with principal AEF general staff officers (May 25, 1919). Left to right: Brig. Gen. Fiske, G-5; Brig. Gen. Andrews, P.M.G.; Maj. Gen. McAndrew, Chief-of-Staff; Brig. Gen. Eltinge, Deputy Chief-of-Staff; Gen. Pershing; Brig. Gen. Nolan, G-2; Brig. Gen. Conner, G-3; Brig. Gen. Davis, A.D.C.; Brig. Gen. Moseley, G-4. Photo taken at AEF GHQ at Chaumont. (US Signal Corps, 159233)

There were sufficient other buildings for the staff and for billets. The French commander was not overjoyed about the arrival of the American headquarters, but the mayor certainly was. The AEF staff was organized following the pattern that existed in the British Army and, generally, within the American military establishment since the reorganisation of the army in 1903. Reporting directly to General Pershing, the commander-in-chief, was his chief-of-staff who coordinated the activities of the "G Staff," that is the officers who directed the various functional divisions of personnel (G-1), intelligence (G-2), operations (G-3), supply (G-4), and training (G-5). At corps and division levels below the AEF, the staff functions of G-3 were combined with those of G-5, and those of G-1 were combined with G-4. The commanding general of the Services of Supply (SOS) also reported through the AEF chief-of-staff. Specialist staff officers included the adjutant general, the inspector general, the judge advocate, the chief of artillery, the chief of the tank corps, and the headquarters commandant, who was responsible for the smooth and efficient operation of the headquarters office. Reporting to General Pershing through Major General James G. Harbord, commander of the SOS from July 29, 1918, to the end of the war, were the chief quartermaster, the chief surgeon, the chief engineer, the chief ordnance officer, the chief signal officer, the chief of the Air Service, the general purchasing agent, the chief of the gas service, the director general of transportation, the Provost Marshal General, and the director of the motor transport corps.

General Harbord pointed out that in an army of two million soldiers a certain number of men "with criminal records" was unavoidable. Accordingly, the military police and military law structure of the AEF/SOS was a critical element in the maintenance of order and discipline in France. Harbord drew on officers with substantial civilian experience in both law enforcement and law to staff those departments. Another important logistical function requiring staff attention at both AEF and SOS levels was purchasing and contracting. Pershing appointed Charles G. Dawes of Chicago to the post of General Purchasing Agent. Millions of tons of shipping were saved by local purchasing throughout the theater of operations. At the end of hostilities the reverse situation became an administrative task of gigantic proportions—disposal of accumulated stores in France. The AEF general staff organization went through progressive changes as the AEF organization matured and expanded, but the basic command and staff relationships remained stable for the remainder of the war.

US flying field at Issoudun, April 1918. Ground crewmen are assembling an aircraft. Issoudun was about 150 miles south of Paris within the SOS Intermediate geographic section. The aviation instruction center with 12 flying fields, the intermediate quartermaster and ammunition depots and a prisoner of war enclosure were located there. (US Signal Corps, 10311)

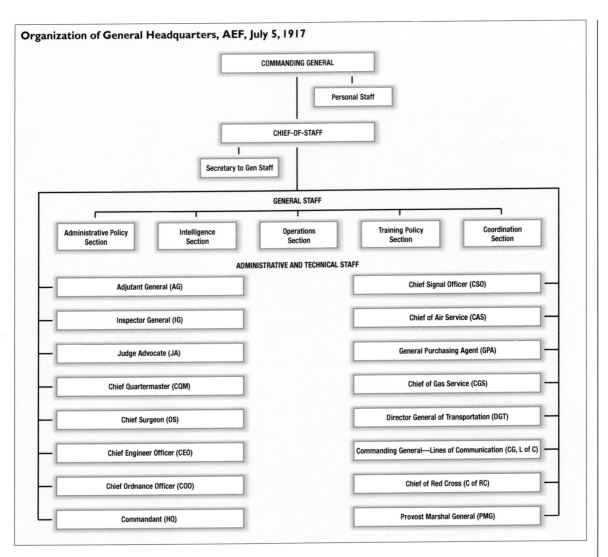

Organization of General Headquarters, AEF, July 5, 1917

COMMANDING GENERAL

Personal Staff

CHIEF-OF-STAFF

Secretary to Gen Staff

GENERAL STAFF

| Administrative Policy Section | Intelligence Section | Operations Section | Training Policy Section | Coordination Section |

ADMINISTRATIVE AND TECHNICAL STAFF

Adjutant General (AG)	Chief Signal Officer (CSO)
Inspector General (IG)	Chief of Air Service (CAS)
Judge Advocate (JA)	General Purchasing Agent (GPA)
Chief Quartermaster (CQM)	Chief of Gas Service (CGS)
Chief Surgeon (OS)	Director General of Transportation (DGT)
Chief Engineer Officer (CEO)	Commanding General—Lines of Communication (CG, L of C)
Chief Ordnance Officer (COO)	Chief of Red Cross (C of RC)
Commandant (HQ)	Provost Marshal General (PMG)

The First Army

It was John Pershing's dream to create an independent field army with US commanders, operating in its own sector of responsibility in France. Some actions had actually preceded the formation of the army itself. Brigadier General Edward F. McGlachlin, Jr. had been designated as chief of artillery of First Army on April 29, 1918, and Brigadier General Benjamin D. Foulois had been appointed as chief of First Army Air Service on May 29, 1918. The American First Army was created on the heels of the successful Aisne–Marne operation to become effective on August 10, 1918.

I and III Corps took responsibility for sectors along the Vesle River from two French corps on August 4 and 5, 1918. It was the first time that two American corps were on line, adjacent to each other in an active battle zone during the war. Field Orders No. 1 confirmed that the American First Army was in command on the Vesle, but Pershing decided that it was not a suitable area to build up the new army. Instead, he, Pétain, and Foch agreed at a conference on August 9 that the Americans should be shifted to the St. Mihiel front. The First Army was to consist of three US corps controlling 14 divisions and the French II Colonial Corps of three divisions. The first battle action of the new American field army was the reduction of the St. Mihiel salient, which had been created during the initial invasion in August 1914.

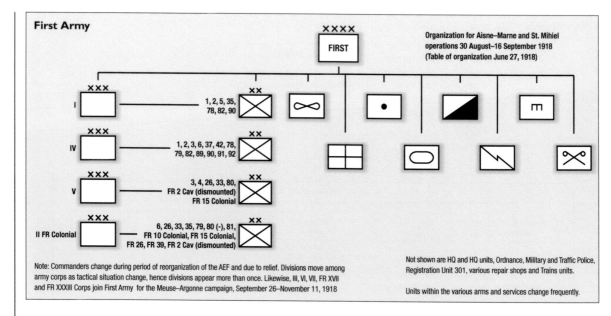

First Army

Organization for Aisne–Marne and St. Mihiel operations 30 August–16 September 1918 (Table of organization June 27, 1918)

I — 1, 2, 5, 35, 78, 82, 90

IV — 1, 2, 3, 6, 37, 42, 78, 79, 82, 89, 90, 91, 92

V — 3, 4, 26, 33, 80, FR 2 Cav (dismounted), FR 15 Colonial

II FR Colonial — 6, 26, 33, 35, 79, 80 (-), 81, FR 10 Colonial, FR 15 Colonial, FR 26, FR 39, FR 2 Cav (dismounted)

Note: Commanders change during period of reorganization of the AEF and due to relief. Divisions move among army corps as tactical situation change, hence divisions appear more than once. Likewise, III, VI, VII, FR XVII and FR XXXIII Corps join First Army for the Meuse–Argonne campaign, September 26–November 11, 1918.

Not shown are HQ and HQ units, Ordnance, Military and Traffic Police, Registration Unit 301, various repair shops and Trains units.

Units within the various arms and services change frequently.

In his final report, General Pershing noted that his forecast in the July 10, 1917, general organization project prepared for the War Department, "that a force of about 1,000,000 is the smallest unit which in modern war will be a complete, well-balanced, and independent fighting organization" proved to be accurate. At the Armistice the AEF had grown to nearly two million soldiers organized into two field armies. A third field army was activated in mid-November 1918.

I Corps

The next large headquarters below the army and above the division was the corps. Army corps had been part of American field army organization since the Civil War, during which they were the standard maneuver unit. Regiments, the basic recruiting and fighting organization, were assigned to brigades and "divisions" within the corps, but those divisions were neither independent nor interchangeable among corps. There were no tables of organization and equipment (TO&E) until July 17, 1862, when Congress directed a corps organization for the army. The standard corps had three divisions "aggregating about 45 regiments of infantry and nine batteries of artillery."

During the Spanish–American war of 1898, seven army corps were authorized, but their strengths varied widely from a low of about 8,000 to a high of nearly 57,000 and they were not uniformly structured. The organization of corps was similar to that in the Civil War, with three regiments in a brigade, three brigades per division and three divisions in the corps. In World War I, corps and armies were not uniform TO&E organizations, apart from their headquarters units, each being tailored to the task at hand. The corps would contain from two to six divisions, which were TO&E organizations. I Army Corps, usually shortened to I Corps, was organized on January 15, 1918, at the direction of the GHQ, AEF. The corps headquarters was situated at Neufchâteau in the Vosges Mountains, 37km south and a bit west from Toul. On January 20, Major General Hunter Liggett assumed command. Liggett was one of the best officers in the army, and certainly in the top echelon of corps and army commanders in the AEF. Despite his unmilitary appearance, somewhat pudgy and disheveled, his capacity for command and his intelligence caused Pershing to rely on him. While commanding the 41st Division that was still in the US awaiting deployment, he and his chief-of-staff, Lieutenant Colonel (later Brigadier General) Malin Craig, "enrolled as students" in order to soak up as much information from the British as possible during a visit to the British Fifth Army in the fall of 1917. Liggett's I Corps consisted of his headquarters, a pioneer infantry regiment, two cavalry regiments, an artillery brigade with two heavy gun or howitzer regiments as well as a 240mm trench mortar battalion, an antiaircraft machine-gun battalion, an observation and sound ranging section, and a corps artillery park. Corps engineer units included a regiment, an engineer train, and a pontoon train. Other units of the corps troops organization included a field signal battalion, a telegraph battalion, a meteorological section, a sanitary train, a mobile veterinary hospital, a military police company, a supply train, a troop transport train, and a remount depot. The total strength of the corps troops organization as specified by the November 1, 1918, B Series TO&E was 21,239, not including the attached combat and depot divisions. The divisions of I Corps during the Meuse–Argonne campaign are shown in the chart immediately below. Although a corps usually had four combat and two depot or replacement divisions, it had 12 US divisions and a French division during the last campaign—a total of about 200,000 soldiers. The battle history of I Corps included the Aisne–Marne campaign, the St. Mihiel campaign and the Meuse–Argonne campaign, where it played a decisive role. Nine US corps were organized during the war, but only the first six sequentially had service prior to the armistice. Three French corps—the II Colonial, the XVII and the XXXIII—served with the AEF in 1918.

Soldier standing atop a Renault light tank to show the relative size of this small fighting machine. This machine mounted the 37mm gun. Others were armed with the Hotchkiss 8mm machine gun. This photo was taken at the US Tank Corps School at Bourg near Langres, France, in July 1918. American-built 6-ton tanks based on the Renault design did not reach France in time to enter combat. (US Signal Corps, 17546)

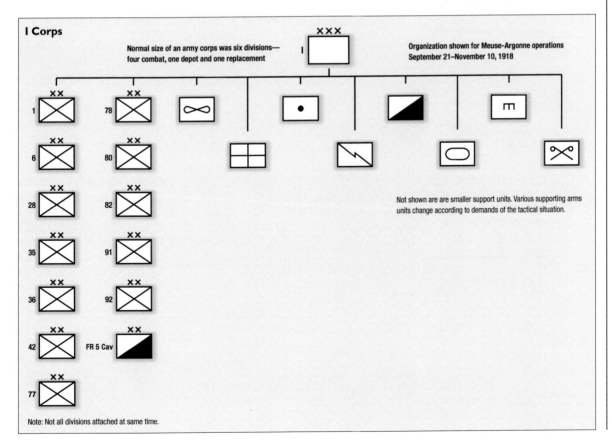

I Corps

Normal size of an army corps was six divisions—four combat, one depot and one replacement

Organization shown for Meuse-Argonne operations September 21–November 10, 1918

Not shown are are smaller support units. Various supporting arms units change according to demands of the tactical situation.

1, 78, 6, 80, 28, 82, 35, 91, 36, 92, 42, FR 5 Cav, 77

Note: Not all divisions attached at same time.

The division

Three categories of infantry divisions were formed by the War Department, each identified by the sources of its soldiers. The Regular Army divisions of the AEF were numbered from 1 to 8, the National Guard divisions from 26 to 42 and the National Army divisions from 76 to 93. Forty-two divisions, not including the 93d, which did not serve as a division (its regiments served with the French Army), arrived for service in France.

Thirteen of those divisions were designated as "replacement," or "depot" divisions, initially allocated two per army corps, but later reduced to one. The depot divisions were pools of replacements for the combat divisions. European armies, notably the German Army, had "depot" units integral to the organization of divisions and army corps. In this way, the early and therefore the most unsettling casualties could be replaced right from within the depleted combat unit itself. American staff planners, quite aware of developments of this sort in Europe, knew that the same dynamic would begin to diminish the combat power, that is the "fighting rifle strength," of US infantry divisions as soon as they entered the line.

The American line division was an infantry organization. Its composition changed from the first Tables of Organization and Equipment (TO&E) of August 8, 1917, with a strength of 27,123 men, right up to June 26, 1918, with 28,059 soldiers. The US division was fully twice the size of any other European division, which suggested some problems of control, movement (the road space to march the division was over 50km), and support. Moreover, the very large division seemed to be the very antithesis of General Pershing's concept of "open" warfare, where maneuver and rifle fire, supported by artillery, was the formula for success in battle. Both the British and French missions that were advising the Americans on matters of organization and procedure believed that the US division was too large and unwieldy. They also were certain that there were far too many soldiers in proportion to the artillery and machine-gun

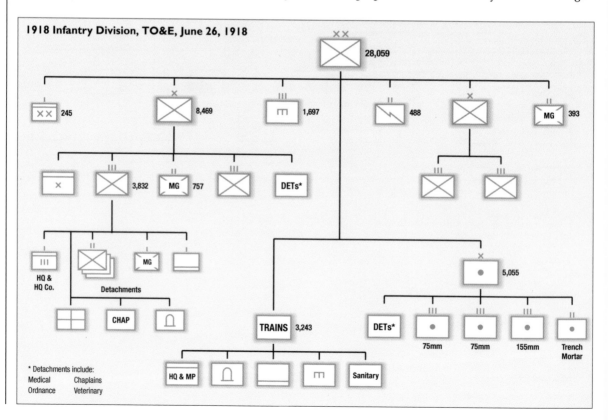

1918 Infantry Division, TO&E, June 26, 1918

28,059 / 245 / 8,469 / 1,697 / 488 / 393 / 3,832 / MG 757 / DETs* / HQ & HQ Co. / Detachments / CHAP / TRAINS 3,243 / HQ & MP / Sanitary / 5,055 / DETs* / 75mm / 75mm / 155mm / Trench Mortar

* Detachments include:
Medical   Chaplains
Ordnance   Veterinary

AEF Divisions [Based on TO&E of August 8, 1917, and June 26. 1918]

Personnel

Unit/Section	8 Aug 1917	Strength	26 Jun 1918	Strength
Division HQ	1	164	1	245
Infantry Brigades	2	8,134 ea	2	8,469 ea
Infantry Regiments	4	3,699 ea	4	3,832 ea
Infantry Battalions	12	1,026 ea	12	1,027 ea
Infantry Brigade MG Bn	1	570	2	757 ea
Regt'l MG Companies	4	178 ea	4	178 ea
Regt'l Supply Companies	4	140 ea	4	160 ea
Regt'l Rifle Companies	48	256 ea	48	256 ea
Field Arty Bde HQ	1	58	1	63
3in. (75mm) Gun Regts	2	1,479 ea	2	1,518 ea
6in. (155mm) How Regt.	1	1,766	1	1,618
Trench Mortar Battery	1	184	1	177
Brigade Medical/Chaplain	–	123 ea	–	127 ea
Brigade Ordnance Dept.	–	20 ea	–	20 ea
Brigade Veterinary Dept.	–	0	–	4 ea
Field Arty Medical/Chaplain	–	102	–	96
Field Arty Ordnance Dept.	–	37	–	49
Field Arty Veterinary Dept.	–	0	–	16
Divison MG Battalion	–	754	–	384
Division MG Bn Medical	–	14	–	7
Division MG Bn Ordnance	–	4	–	2
Engineer Regiment	1	1,634	1	1,660
Engineer Medical/Chaplain	–	32	–	31
Engineer Ordnance	–	6	–	6
Field Signal Battalion	1	262	1	488
Division Aggregate (-Trains)	**1**	**24,243**	**1**	**24,816**
Train HQ and Military Police	1	16	1	374
Ammunition Train	1	1,033	1	1,333
Supply Train	1	472	1	501
Engineer Train	1	84	1	84
Sanitary Train	1	949	1	951
Division Trains total	1	2,880	1	3,243
Division Aggregate (incl. Trains)	**1**	**27,123**	**1**	**28,059**

Note: Strength figures are not mutually exclusive, eg. regimental strengths are included in brigade strengths.

Animals

Unit/Section	8 Aug 1917	Strength	26 Jun 1918	Strength
Draft Horses	–	–	–	1,854
Riding Horses	–	–	–	2,082
Draft Mules	–	–	–	2,565
Pack Mules	–	–	–	55

(continued on page 34)

Riding Mules	–	–	–	82
Total Horses and Mules	–	–	–	6,638

Major Equipment Items

Rolling Kitchens (4-mule)	–	–	–	104
Water Carts (1-mule)	–	–	–	101
Ambulances (4-mule)	–	–	–	13
Combat Carts (1-mule)	–	–	–	300
Arty Battery Wagons (6-horse)	–	–	–	14
Combat Wagons (4-mule/horse)	–	–	–	174
Ration & Baggage Wagons (4-mule)	–	–	–	202
Bicycles	–	–	–	238
Ambulances (Motor)	–	–	–	41
Motor Cars	–	–	–	122
Motorcycles with Sidecar	–	–	–	319
Tractors, $2\frac{1}{2}$ and 5-ton	–	–	–	64
Trucks, all types	–	–	–	577
Artillery Caissons	–	–	–	216
Rifle Grenade Dischargers	–	–	–	1,560
Guns, 3in. or 75mm	–	–	–	50
Guns, 1lb	–	–	–	12
Machine Guns, Antiaircraft	–	–	–	36
Machine Guns, Heavy	–	–	–	224
Howitzers, 6in. or 155mm	–	–	–	24
Trench Knives	–	–	–	1,920
Mortars, Trench	–	–	–	36
Pistols	–	–	–	11,913
Rifles	–	–	–	17,666
Rifles, Automatic	–	–	–	768

Sources: Historical Section, Army War College, Order of Battle of The United States Land Forces in the World War, American Expeditionary Forces, Divisions *(Washington, DC: Government Printing Office, 1931)*, 446–47; United States Army In The World War 1917-1919. Volume 1: Organization of the American Expeditionary Forces *(Washington: Historical Division, Department of the Army, 1948)*

strengths. As it turned out, the large divisions helped to sustain the heavy casualties imposed by fighting straight ahead in the French style. The 29 AEF divisions that eventually participated in combat operations in France consisted of Regulars, National Guardsmen, and National Army soldiers. In 1918 General Peyton C. March, the army's chief-of-staff, eliminated the distinction between these three types.

The 1st Division (Regular)

The 1st Division was formed en passant by directing units that had served in the Punitive Expedition in 1916 to assemble and move to the east coast for shipment to France. It consisted of the 1st and 2d Infantry Brigades and the 1st Artillery Brigade (5th, 6th, and 7th Artillery Regiments). The 16th and 18th Infantry Regiments were assigned to the 1st Brigade, and the 26th and

The 1st Division (Regular Army Infantry Division) (interim appointments not shown)

Commanding Generals

June 8, 1917	Brig. Gen. William L. Sibert (Maj. Gen. after June 27)
December 14, 1917	Maj. Gen. Robert L. Bullard
July 15, 1918	Maj. Gen. Charles P. Summerall
October 18, 1918	Brig. Gen. Frank Parker
November 21, 1918	Maj. Gen. Edward F. McGlachlin, Jr.

Chiefs-of-Staff

June 8, 1917	Col. Frank W. Coe
September 3, 1917	Col. Hanson E. Ely
January 7, 1918	Lt. Col. Campbell King (Col. after June 7)
September 23, 1918	Lt. Col. John N. Greely (Col. after October 17)
November 7, 1918	Col. Stephen O. Fuqua

Commanders, 1st Infantry Brigade 16th and 18th Infantry Regiments; 2d Machine-Gun Battalion

June 9, 1917	Col. Omar Bundy (Brig. Gen. after June 28)
September 3, 1917	Brig. Gen. George B. Duncan
May 5, 1918	Brig. Gen. John L. Hines
August 27, 1918	Brig. Gen. Frank Parker

Commanders, 2d Infantry Brigade 26th and 28th Infantry Regiments; 3d Machine-Gun Battalion

June 7, 1917	Col. Robert L. Bullard (Brig. Gen. after June 28)
September 4, 1917	Brig. Gen. Beaumont B. Buck
August 27, 1918	Brig. Gen. Frank E. Bamford
October 17, 1918	Brig. Gen. George C. Barnhardt
October 26, 1918	Brig. Gen. Francis C. Marshall

Commanders, 1st Field Artillery Brigade 5th (155mm), 6th (75mm) and 7th (75mm) Field Artillery Regiments; 1st Trench Mortar Battery

August 16, 1917	Brig. Gen. Peyton C. March (Maj. Gen. after September 3)
October 12, 1917	Brig. Gen. Charles H. McKinstry
December 23, 1917	Brig. Gen. Charles P. Summerall
August 16, 1918	Col. Henry W. Butner (Brig. Gen. after October 21)

Divisional Troops 1st Machine-Gun Battalion; 1st Engineer Regiment; 2d Field Signal Battalion; Headquarters Troop

Trains 1st Train Headquarters and Military Police; 1st Ammunition Train; 1st Supply Train; 1st Engineer Train; 1st Sanitary Train (Ambulance Companies and Field Hospitals 2, 3, 12, and 13)

(continued on page 36)

Assigned To	
June 26, 1917	GHQ, AEF
October 14, 1917	French Eighth Army
January 5, 1918	French First Army
March 27, 1918	French Eighth Army
April 5, 1918	French Fifth Army
April 17, 1918	French First Army
July 11, 1918	French Tenth Army
July 30, 1918	French Eighth Army
August 24, 1918	US First Army
November 17, 1918	US Third Army
July 2, 1919	US Armed Forces in Germany (AFG)
August 5, 1919	US Services of Supply (SOS)
September, 1919	Division demobilizes at Camp Meade, MD; Headquarters to Camp Taylor, KY for stationing

Source: *Historical Section, Army War College,* Order of Battle of The United States Land Forces in the World War, American Expeditionary Forces, Divisions *(Washington, DC: Government Printing Office, 1931), 1–19.*

Major General Robert L. Bullard, commander of the 1st Division; Colonel Campbell King, chief-of-staff; and Lieutenant Guy Shirey, aide-de-camp, June 30, 1918, at Tartigny in the Cantigny sector. (US Signal Corps, 15832)

28th to the 2d Brigade. The new divisional commander, Major General William Sibert, and the operations officer, Major George C. Marshall, saw each other and their men for the first time on the docks at Hoboken, New Jersey. With nearly 1,000 officers and more than 27,000 enlisted soldiers at maximum strength, the 1st Division was formidable, if not efficient. General Sibert oversaw the initial training of the 1st Division, but was removed by General Pershing in December 1917 in favor of Major General Robert L. Bullard, one of Pershing's favorites.

Bullard had been the commander of the 16th Infantry Regiment during the Punitive Expedition, and the 2d Infantry Brigade upon arrival in France with the 1st Division, but Pershing soon reassigned him to take charge of the AEF schools. Throughout the formative period in France, the 1st Division was held up as the model for other divisions to emulate as they prepared for combat. When the emergency of the German spring offensives of March–April 1918 occurred, Pershing was asked by Foch to provide help. His immediate response was to send the 1st, 2d, and 3d Divisions, all regulars.

The 26th "Yankee" Division (National Guard)

The 26th Division, the "Yankee Division," was a National Guard division that arrived progressively in France in September and October 1917. It was comprised of soldiers from the New England states and organized for deployment at Fort Devens, Massachusetts. The 51st Infantry Brigade (101st and 102d Infantry Regiments) and the 52d Infantry Brigade (103d and 104th Infantry Regiments) were supported by the division's 51st Artillery Brigade (101st, 102d, and 103d Artillery Regiments). Its commander, Major General Clarence Edwards, was a prominent and warm friend of influential New Englanders, despite the fact that he was a regular officer. He graduated from West Point in 1883, three years before his commander-in-chief, John Pershing. As a field grade officer he served in the Philippines on the staff of Major General Henry W. Lawton. In 1906 he received his first star and successive appointments to command two infantry brigades, one on the Mexican border and another in Hawaii. At the entry of the United States into the World War he was commanding the Northeastern Department of the army and was promoted in August to major general.

Major General James McAndrew, the AEF's chief-of-staff, Major General Hunter Liggett, the commander of I Corps, and other regular officers disliked

The 26th Division (National Guard Infantry Division) (interim appointments not shown)

Commanding Generals

August 22, 1917	Maj. Gen. Clarence R. Edwards
October 25, 1918	Brig. Gen. Frank E. Bamford
November 19, 1918	Maj. Gen. Harry C. Hale

Chiefs-of-Staff

August 22, 1917	Lt. Col. George H. Shelton
January 3, 1918	Lt. Col. Cassius M. Dowell
April 18, 1918	Lt. Col. Duncan K. Major, Jr. (Col. after August 12)

Commanders, 51st Infantry Brigade 101st and 102d Infantry Regiments; 102d Machine-Gun Battalion

August 19, 1917	Brig. Gen. Peter E. Traub (Maj. Gen. after July 12, 1918)
July 16, 1918	Brig. Gen. George H. Shelton
November 9, 1918	Col. Hiram I. Bearss, USMC
November 24, 1918	Brig. Gen. Lucius L. Durfee
December 7, 1918	Brig. Gen. George H. Shelton

Commanders, 52d Infantry Brigade 103d and 104th Infantry Regiments; 103d Machine-Gun Battalion

August 20, 1917	Brig. Gen. Charles H. Cole
November 8, 1918	Brig. Gen. George H. Shelton
December 7, 1918	Brig. Gen. Charles H. Cole

Commanders, 51st Field Artillery Brigade 103d (155mm), 101st (75mm) and 102d (75mm) Field Artillery Regiments; 101st Trench Mortar Battery

October 20, 1917	Brig. Gen. William Lassiter
May 9, 1918	Brig. Gen. Dwight E. Aultman
August 19, 1918	Col. Otho W. B. Farr
October 21, 1918	Brig. Gen. Pelham D. Glassford
October 30, 1918	Col. Otho W. B. Farr
November 28, 1918	Brig. Gen. Pelham D. Glassford

Divisional Troops 101st Machine-Gun Battalion; 101st Engineer Regiment; 101st Field Signal Battalion; Headquarters Troop

Trains 101st Train Headquarters and Military Police; 101st Ammunition Train; 101st Supply Train; 101st Engineer Train; 101st Sanitary Train (Ambulance Companies and Field Hospitals 101–104)

Assigned To

October 23, 1917	GHQ, AEF
February 3, 1918	French Sixth Army
March 18, 1918	GHQ, AEF
March 28, 1918	French Eighth Army
June 29, 1918	French Sixth Army

(continued on page 38)

August 13, 1918	GHQ, AEF
August 18, 1918	US First Army
January 25, 1919	US Services of Supply (SOS)
May 3, 1919	Division demobilizes at Camp Devens, MA

Source: *Historical Section, Army War College*, Order of Battle of the United States Land Forces in the World War, American Expeditionary Forces, Divisions *(Washington, DC: Government Printing Office, 1931), 113–29.*

Major General Clarence Edwards, commander of the 26th Division, with Major General Hunter Liggett, commander of I Corps at Toul, May 13, 1918. Edwards, a popular New Englander, was relieved of command by General Pershing during the Meuse–Argonne campaign.
(US Signal Corps, 14608)

Edwards who was in turn adored by his guardsmen. General Edwards was regarded by some as a complainer and excuse-maker. Robert L. Bullard said that he "was so fault-finding and officially critical of our shortcomings" when his 26th Division, "not quite so experienced as ourselves," relieved the 1st Division in the Toul sector on April 1, 1918. As Edward Coffman noted in his history of the American experience in World War I, there was some friction between Regular Army and National Guard officers, the latter being judged by the former as amateurs in uniform. During the St. Mihiel operation, near the end of the first day, the Yankee Division was ordered to push hard to meet the 1st Division attack at Vigneulles. It met its timetable and showed its flexibility and fighting power. When the commander-in-chief relieved Edwards on October 22, 1918, during the Meuse–Argonne campaign, the New England media cried foul. Edwards was not the only division commander fired by Pershing, only the most vocal and political. The Yankee Division was a good outfit that served in all major campaigns and stood near the top of the list of units that captured Germans and sustained battle casualties.

As might be expected the unit histories of the 26th had a different take on the division's relationship with GHQ. War correspondent Bert Ford who accompanied the division to France, noted that "the rank and file of National Guardsmen in France accused the regular army officers of exercising a 'military autocracy every bit as severe as anything in vogue in Germany.'" When Pershing removed Edwards at "the height of operations … it caused a hurricane of surprise and regret." Ford repeated the familiar epithet that it was all because the Regular Army held a "grudge" against the National Guard. Ford pointed out that sort of talk was commonplace among the troops and even "increased tremendously after the armistice" when there was time to "think and find fault and when open criticism was not likely to affect the success of the cause." The soldiers of the Yankee Division, whether newest recruit or most grizzled veteran, praised their commanding general to the point of worship. "This sentiment was not exaggerated. I talked with the men," said Ford, "and I know … Those were dark days for the 26th." The commanders of the 101st and 103d Infantry Regiments and the 52d Infantry Brigade were also relieved in the following weeks. General Pershing subsequently reinstated all three.

The 77th "Metropolitan" (or "Liberty") Division (National Army)
The 77th Division consisted of soldiers from New York City and was organized at Camp Upton, New York, for overseas service. It arrived in France in April and May 1918, the first National Army division in the theater of operations. The division comprised the 153d Infantry Brigade (305th and 306th Infantry Regiments), the 154th Infantry Brigade (307th and 308th Infantry Regiments) and the 152nd Artillery Brigade (304th, 305th, and 306th Artillery Regiments). Major General Robert Alexander took command on August 27, 1918, following others who had organized and trained the National Army division. It was General Alexander's task to root out the Germans from the tangled and lethal defensive positions of the Argonne Forest in October, after his division had undergone training with the British army and had seen active service in Lorraine in July and along the Vesle and Aisne rivers in August.

The 77th Division (National Army Infantry Division) (interim appointments not shown)

Commanding Generals

August 18, 1917	Maj. Gen. J. Franklin Bell
May 8, 1918	Maj. Gen. George B. Duncan
August 27, 1918	Maj. Gen. Robert Alexander

Chiefs-of-Staff

August 20, 1917	Lt. Col. Ewing E. Booth (Col. after March 26, 1918)
July 11, 1918	Col. John R. R. Hannay
October 11, 1918	Col. Clarence O. Sherrill
December 5, 1918	Lt. Col. John J. Burleigh

Commanders, 153d Infantry Brigade 305th and 306th Infantry Regiments; 305th Machine-Gun Battalion

August 27, 1917	Brig. Gen. Edmund Wittenmyer
October 26, 1918	Brig. Gen. William R. Smedberg, Jr.
November 4, 1918	Brig. Gen. Michael J. Lenihan

Commanders, 154th Infantry Brigade 307th and 308th Infantry Regiments; 306th Machine-Gun Battalion

August 27, 1917	Brig. Gen. Evan M. Johnson
September 9, 1918	Brig. Gen. Edmund Wittenmyer
September 25, 1918	Brig. Gen. Evan M. Johnson
October 30, 1918	Brig. Gen. Harrison J. Price

Commanders, 152d Field Artillery Brigade 306th (155mm), 304th (75mm) and 305th (75mm) Field Artillery Regiments; 302d Trench Mortar Battery

October 16, 1917	Brig. Gen. John D. Barrette
February 7, 1918	Brig. Gen. Thomas H. Rees
August 5, 1918	Col. Manus McCloskey (Brig. Gen. after December 8, 1918)

Divisional Troops 304th Machine-Gun Battalion; 302d Engineer Regiment; 302d Field Signal Battalion; Headquarters Troop

Trains 302nd Train Headquarters and Military Police; 302d Ammunition Train; 302d Supply Train; 302d Engineer Train; 302d Sanitary Train (Ambulance Companies and Field Hospitals 305–308

Assigned To

April 12, 1918	GHQ, AEF
April 15, 1918	British Second Army
May 14, 1918	British Third Army
June 6, 1918	French Eighth Army
August 6, 1918	French Sixth Army
September 8, 1918	French Fifth Army
September 17, 1918	French Second Army
September 22, 1918	US First Army
February 12, 1919	US Services of Supply (SOS)
May 9, 1919	Division demobilizes at Camp Upton, NY (Long Island)

Source: Historical Section, Army War College, Order of Battle of the United States Land Forces in the World War, American Expeditionary Forces, Divisions (Washington, DC: Government Printing Office, 1931), 296-307.

39

26th Division troops in trucks near Menil-la-Tour, April 1, 1918. The Yankee Division was one of the early divisions deployed to France. (US Signal Corps, 12007)

Perhaps the best-known action of the division was in the Argonne Forest. The 77th, along with the 28th and the 35th National Guard divisions, was part of Major General Hunter Liggett's I Corps. The 92d Division was in corps reserve at the outset of the Meuse–Argonne campaign on September 26, 1918. The 77th had about 6.5km of rugged, forested terrain in its zone.

A composite battalion-sized group of soldiers from two battalions of the 308th Infantry Regiment and two companies of the 306th Machine-Gun Battalion were cut off and isolated for five days near Charlevaux Mill. Major Charles Whittlesey, commander of the 1st Battalion, 308th Infantry Regiment, was the senior officer. General Alexander, in his account in the division's unit history, stated that he realized the "extremely critical" situation faced by his troops. Efforts to resupply and maintain communication with the detachment were foiled by "the density of the undergrowth" and the uncertainty of its exact location in the forest. Two airplanes and their pilots were lost in the efforts. The relief forces from the division reached the little band on the night of October 7 and discovered that there were only about 35 percent effectives from the original group of 554 men.

General Alexander, perhaps not the most objective observer, did assess the training of his junior officers and noncommissioned officers as they left the Vesle River front for the Argonne as leaving "much to be desired." In particular, their ability to "combine movement with fire" was deficient. He attributed this to a "lack of time" to train properly for open warfare. Alexander also found fault with the complex organization of the infantry regiment—"more complicated than the abilities of the average colonel permit him to use effectively." He also favored placing several light artillery pieces with the regiment to blast out enemy machine-gun positions, and believed that the medium 155mm artillery should be motorized to improve mobility and flexibility of fire planning. Similarly, he argued for "four or five planes" to be added to the division organization to facilitate continual training with the ground troops. Partly because the 77th was given such a wide frontage to deal with in the Argonne, General Alexander concluded that the three brigades of three infantry regiments each that were the core of the "fighting rifle strength" of the initial division TO&E in 1917 should be restored. Clearly the 77th, formed from American citizen levies in the historic spirit of the militia of the United States, fought bravely and well in France.

Statistical comparison

The three divisions highlighted in this chapter were combat infantry divisions. The 1st began to arrive on June 26, 1917, then served 127 days in quiet sectors and 93 days in active sectors, the longest time of any of the 29 combat divisions. The 26th arrived sequentially in France in September and October 1917, after receiving a "transfusion" of 900 soldiers from the 76th Division. The Yankee Division served 148 days in quiet sectors and 45 in active sectors. The 77th Division organized at Camp Upton, New York, where it both received soldiers from and provided soldiers to other divisions. The division began deployment in March 1918 and closed in France on May 13. The Metropolitan (Liberty) Division served 47 days in quiet sectors and 66 days in active sectors.

The 77th Division made the greatest advance against the enemy—71.5km, followed by the 1st at 51km and the 26th with 37km. The 1st captured 6,469 Germans, the 26th took 3,148, and the 77th got 750. The 1st Division had 4,411 men killed in action and 17,201 wounded (total 21,612), the 26th had 2,135 soldiers killed and 11,325 wounded (total 13,460), and the 77th accumulated 1,992 killed and 8,505 wounded (10,497 total). Those three divisions were in the top nine of the 29 combat divisions in France. The grand total for the AEF was 50,280 battle deaths and 205,690 wounded. An additional 46 men were missing and 4,480 were taken prisoner. As expected, the infantry and machine-gun units took most of the casualties, between 50 and 80 percent. Of the 14 belligerents that suffered casualties, only Greece and Portugal lost fewer men than the United States.

The division infantry brigade

The combat soldiers of the American division were organized into two infantry brigades of 8,469 men each. The brigade consisted of two infantry regiments, each with 3,768 soldiers, a brigade headquarters of 25 soldiers, a machine-gun battalion of 757 soldiers and supporting medical, ordnance, and veterinary field units, along with a group of chaplains. The four infantry regiments of the

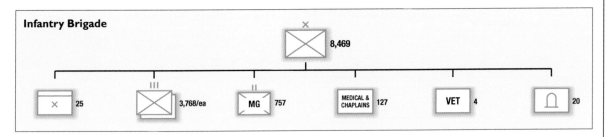

A USMC sentry stands guard during a gas attack at the Post of Command (PC) of the 4th Brigade, 2d Division, east of Verdun, March 27, 1918. Note the mule-drawn water trailer ("water buffalo"), which may have been contaminated by the gas. The 5th Marines occupied the sector named "Moscow" by the French. (US Signal Corps, 12163)

AEF Infantry Brigades (Based on TO&E of June 26, 1918)

Personnel

Unit/Section	26 Jun 1918	Strength
Brigade HQ	1	25
Infantry Regiments	2	3,768 ea
Machine-Gun Battalion	1	757
Total Combatants	–	**8,318**
Medical Dept. & Chaplains	–	127
Ordnance Dept.	–	20
Veterinary Field Unit	–	4
Brigade Aggregate	1	**8,469**

Note: Strength figures are not mutually exclusive, e.g. regimental strengths are included in brigade strengths.

Animals

Draft Mules	–	821
Riding Horses	–	185
Riding Mules	–	33
Total Horses and Mules	–	**1,039**

Major Equipment Items

Rolling Kitchens (4-mule)	–	36
Water Carts (1-mule)	–	34
Combat Carts (1-mule)	–	150
Medical Carts (1-mule)	–	7
Ration Carts (2-mule)	–	37
Combat Wagons (4-mule/horse)	–	46
Ration & Baggage Wagons (4-mule)	–	50
Bicycles	–	94
Motor Cars	–	3
Motorcycles with Sidecar	–	8
Rifle Grenade Dischargers	–	780
Guns, 1lb	–	6
Machine Guns, Heavy	–	96
Trench Knives	–	960
Mortars, 3in. Stokes	–	12
Pistols	–	3,183
Rifles	–	6,457
Rifles, Automatic	–	384

Note: There are some discrepancies between this brigade list and the brigade section of the division list. Both lists are part of the same TO&E of 26 June 1918.

Sources: United States Army In The World War 1917–1919. Volume 1: Organization of the American Expeditionary Forces (Washington: Historical Division, Department of the Army, 1948)

Infantry Regiment

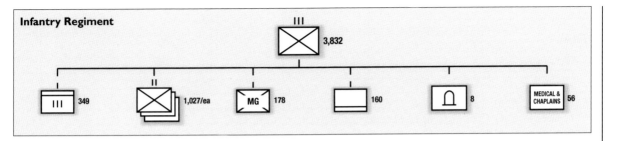

AEF Infantry Regiments (Based on TO&E of June 26, 1918)		
Personnel		
Unit/Section	**26 Jun 1918**	**Strength**
Regimental HQ & HQ Co.	I	349
Infantry Battalions	3	1,027 ea
Machine-Gun Company	I	178
Supply Company	I	160
Total Combatants	–	**3,768**
Medical Dept. & Chaplains	–	56
Ordnance Dept.	–	8
Regiment Aggregate	I	**3,832**
Animals		
Draft Mules	–	315
Riding Horses	–	65
Riding Mules	–	10
Total Horses and Mules	–	**390**
Major Equipment Items		
Rolling Kitchens (4-mule)	–	16
Water Carts (1-mule)	–	15
Combat Carts (1-mule)	–	27
Medical Carts (1-mule)	–	3
Ration Carts (2-mule)	–	16
Combat Wagons (4-mule)	–	19
Ration & Baggage Wagons (4-mule)	–	22
Bicycles	–	42
Motor Cars	–	1
Motorcycles with Sidecar	–	2
Rifle Grenade Dischargers	–	390
Guns, 1lb	–	3
Machine Guns, Heavy	–	16
Trench Knives	–	480
Mortars, 3in. Stokes	–	6

(continued on page 44)

Pistols	–	1,200
Rifles	–	3,200
Rifles, Automatic	–	192

Note: There are some discrepancies between this regimental list and the brigade and division lists. All are part of the same TO&E of June 26, 1918.
Source: *United States Army In The World War 1917–1919. Volume 1: Organization of the American Expeditionary Forces (Washington: Historical Division, Department of the Army, 1948)*

Infantry Battalion

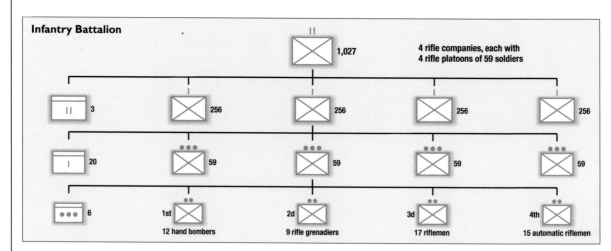

4 rifle companies, each with 4 rifle platoons of 59 soldiers

12 hand bombers · 9 rifle grenadiers · 17 riflemen · 15 automatic riflemen

AEF Infantry Rifle Companies (Based on TO&E of 26 June 1918)

Personnel

Unit/Section	26 Jun 1918	Strength
Company HQ	1	20
Infantry Platoon	4	59 ea
Total Combatants	**–**	**256**
Platoon HQ	4	6 ea
1st Section—Hand Bombers	4	12 ea
2d Section—Rifle Grenadiers	4	9 ea
3d Section—Riflemen	4	17 ea
4th Section—Automatic Riflemen	4	15 ea
Platoon Aggregate	**4**	**59 ea**

Animals

Draft Mules	–	15 *

*Mules furnished on order, not organic to company.

Major Equipment Items

Rolling Kitchens (4-mule)	–	1 [from supply company]
Water Carts (1-mule)	–	1 [from supply company]
Ration Carts (2-mule)	–	1 [from supply company]

44 | *(continued on page 45)*

Combat Wagons (4-mule)	–	1 [from supply company]
Ration & Baggage Wagons (4-mule)	–	1 [from supply company}
Rifle Grenade Dischargers	–	30
Trench Knives	–	40
Pistols	–	73
Rifles	–	235
Rifles, Automatic	–	16 [8 in platoons, 8 co. reserve]

Note: There are some discrepancies between this company/platoon list and other lists. All are part of the same TO&E of June 26, 1918.
Sources: United States Army In The World War 1917–1919. Volume 1: Organization of the American Expeditionary Forces *(Washington: Historical Division, Department of the Army, 1948)*

division, each comprising 3,832 soldiers (64 medical, chaplain, and ordnance troops attached from brigade assets to the 3,768 base strength), included a headquarters and headquarters company of 349 soldiers, three infantry battalions of 1,027 soldiers each, a machine-gun company of 178 soldiers, and a supply company of 160 men. The three infantry battalions of each infantry regiment consisted of 1,027 men organized into a headquarters company and four rifle companies. The infantry battalion was a pure fighting infantry unit. All of the supporting fires from artillery, machine guns, and mortars came from other units above the battalion. Each rifle company consisted of a headquarters section of 20 soldiers and four rifle platoons, each with 59 soldiers. The rifle platoon had a headquarters section of six men and four sections, each with a slightly different function. The 1st section consisted of 12 hand bombers; the 2d section had nine rifle grenadiers; the 3d section had 17 riflemen; and the 4th section had 15 automatic riflemen.

The division artillery brigade

Combat power within the division was generated by "fighting rifle" strength and supporting fires from light and heavy artillery regiments, machine-gun battalions and companies and trench mortar batteries. The field artillery brigade of the division was a robust organization. The main firepower was delivered by the two light artillery regiments, each consisting of 1,518 soldiers and 24 75mm guns. The heavy artillery regiment consisted of 1,618 men and 24 155mm howitzers. Both the light and heavy guns were of French manufacture. The major organizational difference between the light and heavy regiments was the number of battalions and batteries within each type of regiment. The 75mm-gun light regiments each had two battalions of three four-gun batteries. The 155mm howitzer regiment had

French children watch American soldiers draw a 155mm gun into position at the AEF Tractor and Artillery School, St. Maur, Paris, May 9, 1918. (US Signal Corps, 11980)

Field Artillery Brigade

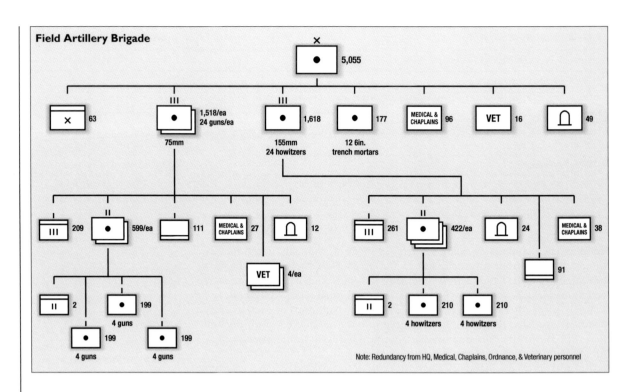

Note: Redundancy from HQ, Medical, Chaplains, Ordnance, & Veterinary personnel

AEF Field Artillery Brigades (Based on TOE of 26 June 1918)

Personnel

Unit/Section	26 Jun 1918	Strength
Brigade HQ	1	63
3in. Gun Regiments	2	1,518 ea
6in. Howizer Regiment	1	1,618
Trench Mortar Battery	1	177
Total combatants	–	**4,894**
Medical Dept. & Chaplains	–	96
Ordnance Dept.	–	49
Veterinary Field Unit	–	16
Brigade Aggregate	1	**5,055**

Note: Strength figures are not mutually exclusive, e.g. regimental strengths are included in brigade strengths.

Animals

Draft Horses	–	1,458
Riding Horses	–	925
Riding Mules	–	16
Draft Mules	–	318
Total Horses and Mules	–	**2,717**

Major Equipment Items

Rolling Kitchens (4-mule & Trail)	–	25

 (continued on page 47)

Water Carts (1-mule)	–	16
Battery Reel Carts (2-horse)	–	12
Regt/Bn Reel Carts	–	11
Medical Carts (1-mule)	–	4
Ration Carts (2-mule)	–	17
Battery Wagons (6-horse)	–	12
Comb. Store/Bty Wagons (6-horse)	–	2
Ration & Baggage Wagons (4-mule)	–	48
Spring Wagons (2-horse)	–	4
Store Wagons (6-horse)	–	12
Bicycles	–	26
Motor Ambulance	–	3
Motor Cars	–	28
Reconnaissance Cars	–	6
Motorcycles with Sidecar	–	117
Ordnance Tractors (2.5-ton)	–	4
Ordnance Tractors (5-ton)	–	60
Trucks, Cargo	–	18
Trucks, Ammunition	–	104
Trucks, Artillery Repair	–	3
Trucks, Reel & Fire Control	–	6
Truck, Light Repair	–	1
Trucks, Supply	–	14
Trucks, Tank	–	3
Trucks, Telephone	–	4
Trucks, Wireless	–	3
Caissons	–	180
Guns (3in. or 75mm)	–	48
Howitzers (6in. or 155mm)	–	24
Machine Guns, Antiaircraft	–	36
Trench Mortars (6in.)	–	12
Pistols	–	3,620
Rifles	–	1,339

Sources: United States Army In The World War 1917–1919. Volume 1: Organization of the American Expeditionary Forces (*Washington: Historical Division, Department of the Army, 1948*)

Field Artillery Regiment (Light)

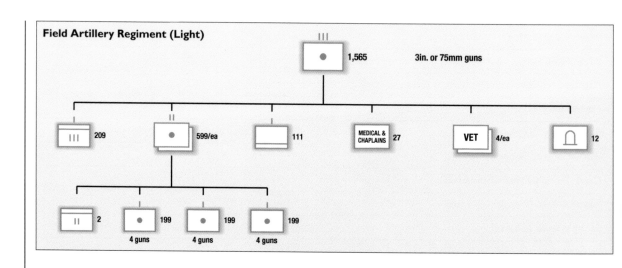

AEF Field Artillery Light Regiments (Based on TO&E of 26 June 1918)

Personnel

Unit/Section	26 Jun 1918	Strength
Regimental HQ	1	4
Battalion HQ	2	2 ea
Regimental HQ Company	1	205
Regimental Supply Company	1	111
Firing Batteries	6	199 ea
Total Combatants	–	**1,518**
Medical Dept. & Chaplains	–	27
Ordnance Dept.	–	12
Veterinary Field Unit	2	4 ea
Regiment Aggregate	1	**1,565**

Animals

Draft Horses	–	726
Riding Horses	–	407
Riding Mules	–	8
Draft Mules	–	152
Total Horses and Mules	–	**1,293**

Major Equipment Items

Rolling Kitchens (4-mule)	–	8
Water Carts (1-mule)	–	8
Battery Reel Carts (2-horse)	–	6
Regt/Bn Reel Carts	–	3
Medical Carts (1-mule)	–	2
Ration Carts (2-mule)	–	8
Battery Wagons (6-horse)	–	6

 (continued on page 49)

Comb. Store/Bty Wagons (6-horse)	–	1
Ration & Baggage Wagons (4-mule)	–	23
Spring Wagons (2-horse)	–	2
Store Wagons (6-horse)	–	6
Bicycles	–	12
Motor Car	–	1
Motorcycles with Sidecar	–	3
Truck, Telephone	–	1
Truck, Wireless	–	1
Caissons (6-horse)	–	72
Guns (3in. or 75mm)[6-horse]	–	24
Machine Guns, Antiaircraft	–	12
Pistols	–	1,451
Rifles	–	87

Note: Regimental totals may not agree with field artillery brigade list numbers because some units/personnel are listed separately rather than with the regiments. Light regiments comprised 2 battalions (3, 4-gun batteries each).
Source: United States Army In The World War 1917–1919. Volume 1: Organization of the American Expeditionary Forces (Washington: Historical Division, Department of the Army, 1948)

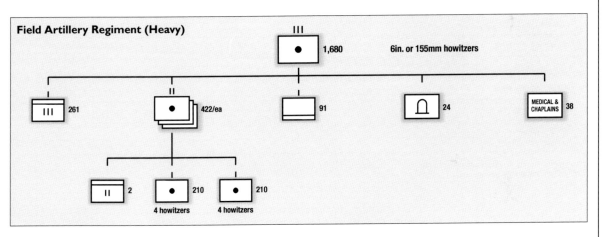

Field Artillery Regiment (Heavy)

6in. or 155mm howitzers

4 howitzers   4 howitzers

This is the training that the French children were observing. (US Signal Corps, 11981)

AEF Field Artillery Heavy Regiments (Based on TO&E of June 26, 1918)

Personnel

Unit/Section	26 Jun 1918	Strength
Regimental HQ	1	4
Battalion HQ	3	2 ea
Regimental HQ Company	1	257
Regimental Supply Company	1	91
Firing Batteries	6	210 ea
Total Combatants	–	**1,618**
Medical Dept. & Chaplains	–	38
Ordnance Dept.	–	24
Regiment Aggregate	1	**1,680**

Major Equipment Items

Rolling Kitchens (Trail)	–	8
Ambulances, motor	–	3
Tractors, Ordnance 2.5-ton	–	4
Regt/Bn Reel Carts	–	4
Tractors, Ordnance 5-ton	–	60
Trucks, Cargo	–	16
Trucks, Ammunition	–	95
Trucks, Artillery Repair	–	3
Trucks, Reel and Fire Control	–	6
Truck, Repair, Light	–	1
Trucks, Supply	–	13
Trucks, Tank	–	3
Cars, Motor, all types		29
Motorcycles with Sidecar		108
Truck, Telephone	–	1
Truck, Wireless	–	1
Caissons	–	36
Howitzers (6in. or 155mm)	–	24
Guns, Machine, Anti-Aircraft	–	12
Pistols	–	597 (incl 14 from attached units)
Rifles	–	1,045

Note: The heavy field artillery regiments comprised three battalions (two batteries each), whereas the light field artillery regiments comprised two battalions (three batteries each).

Source: *United States Army In The World War 1917–1919. Volume 1: Organization of the American Expeditionary Forces (Washington: Historical Division, Department of the Army, 1948)*

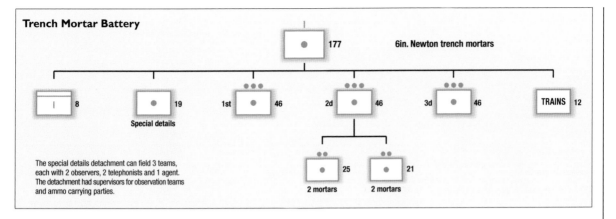

Trench Mortar Battery

177 — 6in. Newton trench mortars

8 | 19 Special details | 1st 46 | 2d 46 | 3d 46 | TRAINS 12

2d: 25 — 2 mortars | 21 — 2 mortars

The special details detachment can field 3 teams, each with 2 observers, 2 telephonists and 1 agent. The detachment had supervisors for observation teams and ammo carrying parties.

three battalions of two four-gun batteries. This provided 72 artillery pieces within the divisional artillery that the division commander could use to weight the battle. A trench mortar battery of 177 men and 12 6in. mortars was also "organic" to the artillery brigade. In addition to this immediately available firepower, the division commander could call upon additional artillery support from corps and army.

The Air Service

Aviation with troops had its beginning in the Signal Corps of the army. Eight training airplanes had accompanied Brigadier General Pershing's punitive expedition into Mexico in 1916, but they soon were inoperative with no means to repair or maintain them in the field. As the AEF was formed provision was made on September 3, 1917, for a chief of the Air Service, independent of the Signal Corps, in the GHQ organization. In accordance with a major reorganization of the GHQ in February 1918, all the technical services were moved under the control of the Services of Supply (SOS) at Tours. The chief of the Air Service maintained a staff position at Chaumont to advise the commander-in-chief on the general employment of air assets while the administration and logistics for the service were handled from Tours, eventually under an assistant chief of the Air Service. Lieutenant Colonel William "Billy" Mitchell, who served as chief in June to August 1917, was followed by Brigadier General Benjamin D. Foulois from the fall of 1917 to the spring of 1918 when he turned his office over to Brigadier General Mason M. Patrick, a West Point classmate of Pershing, who controlled air operations until the end of the war. Foulois was an early pioneer of military aviation, but Patrick was an able staff administrator whom Pershing used in many capacities, which was important as the air arm of the AEF grew larger. The Air Service staff coordinated closely with the Engineer Division of Construction and Forestry to select and develop the airfields serving the AEF. By August 1918 the Air Service

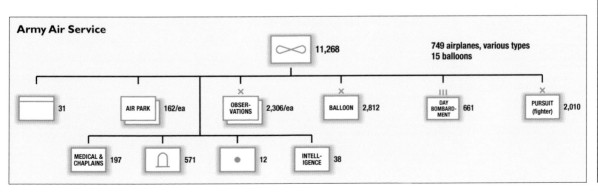

Army Air Service

11,268 — 749 airplanes, various types / 15 balloons

31 | AIR PARK 162/ea | OBSERVATIONS 2,306/ea | BALLOON 2,812 | DAY BOMBARDMENT 661 | PURSUIT (fighter) 2,010

MEDICAL & CHAPLAINS 197 | 571 | 12 | INTELLIGENCE 38

AEF Army Air Services (Based on TO&E of September 8, 1918)

Personnel

Unit/Section	Number	Strength
Headquarters	1	31
Air Parks (airfields)	2	162 ea
Army Observation Wings	2	2,306 ea
Balloon Wing	1	2,812
Monoplace Pursuit Wing *	1	2,010
Day Bombardment Group	1	661
Air Service Combatants	**–**	**10,450**
Med. Dept. & Chaplains	–	197
Ordnance Dept.	–	571
Artillery	–	12
Intelligence	–	38
Air Service Aggregate	**–**	**11,268**

* Monoplace Pursuit aircraft are single-seat, fighter planes. Although the word "monoplace" appears to be a misspelling of "monoplane," the TO&E and other references use monoplace and bi-place to describe the two basic types of aircraft, i.e. one-seat and two-seat.

Major Equipment Items

Ambulances, Motor	–	10
Motor Cars	–	167
Motor Cars, Light	–	30
Motorcycles with Sidecars	–	423
Motorcycles	–	36
Motor Trucks (3-ton)	–	318
Motor Trucks (3-ton, 4-wheel drive)	–	90
Motor Trucks, Repair	–	68
Motor Trucks (1½-ton)	–	382
Motor Trucks, Lighting	–	7
Motor Trucks, Photo	–	8
Motor trucks, Radio	–	10
Motor Trucks, Winch	–	15
Motor Trucks, Tender	–	15
Trailers (3-ton)	–	135
Trailers (1½-ton)	–	204
Trailers (1-ton)	–	220
Trailers, Rolling Kitchen	–	30
Trailers, Photo	–	8
Trailers, Radio	–	10
Trailers, Water Tank	–	15
Airplanes	–	749
Balloons	–	15
Pistols	–	2,929

 (continued on page 53)

Rifles	–	8,136
Rifles, Automatic	–	15
Machine Guns, AA-Mount	–	90
Machine Guns, Synchronized	–	1,578
Machine Guns, Flexible	–	1,102

Source: United States Army In The World War 1917–1919. Volume 1: Organization of the American Expeditionary Forces *(Washington: Historical Division, Department of the Army, 1948)*

Pursuit (Fighter) Squadron

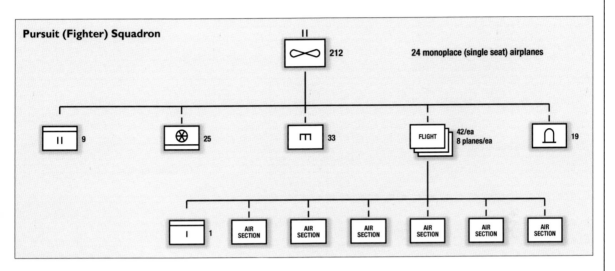

24 monoplace (single seat) airplanes

AEF Pursuit [Fighter] Squadron, Air Service (Based on TO&E of September 8, 1918)

Personnel

Unit/Section	Number	Strength
Headquarters (1st section)	1	9
Supply & Trans. (2d section)	1	25
Engineering (3d section)	1	33
Flights	3	42 ea
Air Sections (6 per flight)	18	126 total
Total Combatants	–	**193**
Ordnance Dept.	–	19
Squadron Aggregate	–	**212**

Note: Some duplication in figures, e.g. air section numbers and flight numbers not mutually exclusive. The pursuit wing consisted of three groups, each with three squadrons. The AEF Air Service had one pursuit wing. As the AEF expanded, the Air Service units increased.

Major Equipment Items

Motor Cars	–	2
Motor Car, Light	–	1
Motorcycles with Sidecars	–	7
Motorcycles	–	1

(continued on page 54)

Motor Trucks (3-ton)	–	7
Motor Trucks, Repair	–	2
Motor Trucks (1½-ton)	–	9
Trailers (3-ton)	–	4
Trailers (1½-ton)	–	3
Trailers (1-ton)	–	9
Trailer, Rolling Kitchen	–	1
Airplanes	–	25
Pistols	–	63
Rifles	–	149
Machine Guns, Synchronized	–	52

Source: United States Army In The World War 1917–1919. Volume 1: Organization of the American Expeditionary Forces *(Washington: Historical Division, Department of the Army, 1948)*

Observation Squadron

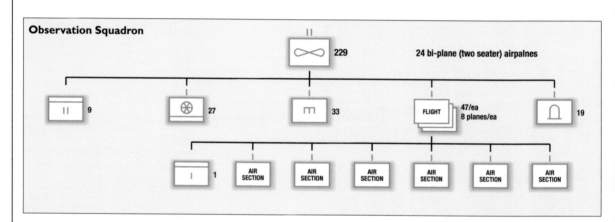

AEF Observation Squadron, Air Service (Based on TO&E of September 8, 1918)

Personnel

Unit/Section	Number	Strength
Headquarters (1st section)	1	9
Supply & Trans. (2d section)	1	27
Engineering (3d section)	1	33
Flights	3	47 ea
Total Combatants	**–**	**210**
Ordnance Dept.	–	19
Squadron Aggregate	**–**	**229**

Note: Some duplication in figures, e.g. air section numbers and flight numbers not mutually exclusive.

Major Equipment Items

Motor Cars	–	4
Motor Car, Light	–	1
Motorcycles with Sidecars	–	10

 (continued on page 55)

Motorcycle	–	1
Motor Trucks (3-ton)	–	7
Motor Trucks, Repair	–	2
Motor Trucks (1½-ton)	–	9
Trailers (3-ton)	–	4
Trailers (1½-ton)	–	3
Trailers (1-ton)	–	9
Trailer, Rolling Kitchen	–	1
Airplanes	–	24
Pistols	–	75
Rifles	–	154
Machine guns, Synchronized	–	50
Machine guns, Flexible	–	50

Source: United States Army In The World War 1917–1919. Volume 1: Organization of the American Expeditionary Forces *(Washington: Historical Division, Department of the Army, 1948)*

strength in SOS had risen to nearly 56,000. The Air Service assets with the army consisted of 11,268 soldiers and 749 airplanes, organized into two air parks (fields), two observation wings, one balloon wing, one monoplane pursuit wing, and a day bombardment group. A wing consisted of three groups, a group had three (some sources say four) squadrons. An air park, which was relatively small (162 personnel), had the essential technicians and food service personnel for the Air Service units. The air assets with army corps were 1,725 personnel and 76 airplanes. An observation group (694 men and 73 airplanes) was comprised of three (some sources say four) squadrons. A balloon group of 932 soldiers and five balloons also supported the corps.

The Tank Corps

The organization of the American tank forces in World War I was largely an ad hoc affair. The armored fighting vehicle was an invention contemporaneous with the Great War. Tactical systems governing its employment in battle had to be formulated on the battlefields of the Somme by trial and error. Although the Holt tractor with its caterpillar track suspension had been adapted by the British

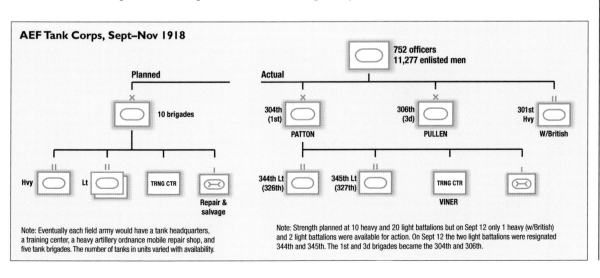

AEF Tank Corps, Sept–Nov 1918

752 officers
11,277 enlisted men

Planned — 10 brigades

Actual — 304th (1st) PATTON; 306th (3d) PULLEN; 301st Hvy W/British

Hvy / Lt / TRNG CTR / Repair & salvage

344th Lt (326th) / 345th Lt (327th) / TRNG CTR VINER

Note: Eventually each field army would have a tank headquarters, a training center, a heavy artillery ordnance mobile repair shop, and five tank brigades. The number of tanks in units varied with availability.

Note: Strength planned at 10 heavy and 20 light battalions but on Sept 12 only 1 heavy (w/British) and 2 light battalions were available for action. On Sept 12 the two light battalions were resigned 344th and 345th. The 1st and 3d brigades became the 304th and 306th.

soldier-inventor Sir Ernest Swinton and others to the problems of mechanized warfare, it was yet to be worked out whether the tank was best suited as an independent arm or an infantry support unit.

The American Tank Service (later renamed Tank Corps) was established by the War Department in January 1918 with Colonel Ira C. Wellborn in command. In France, General Pershing appointed Colonel Samuel D. Rockenbach chief of the AEF Tank Corps in December 1917. The AEF Tank Corps operated independently from the US Tank Service throughout World War I. Captain George S. Patton, who was serving as Headquarters Troop commander at GHQ in Chaumont in the fall of 1917, was assigned to Rockenbach's command at the school center at Langres in December 1917. Patton and his main assistant, Lieutenant Elgin Braine, were charged with the organization of the new school for light tank tactics at Bourg, just a few kilometers from Langres. Training for heavy tanks was to be centered in the US and at Bovington in England.

Shortly after taking office the new army chief-of-staff, Major General Peyton C. March acted decisively to stimulate the growth of the Tank Corps and moved to solve several other difficult organizational issues that had been puzzling the War Department General Staff for months. The original impetus, however, had come from General Pershing, who paid attention to the reports of Major Frank Parker, who had observed French tank operations in the spring of 1917. On July 11, Pershing approved his General Organization Project (GOP) for the AEF and sent the recommendation to the War Department. He had avoided a conflict between the Chauncey Baker Board, sent by the War Department to study British and French equipment and methods, and his own AEF General Staff by convening a conference in Paris to work out the differences and to "exchange ideas." Organization of a Tank Corps in the AEF had not been addressed in the GOP, except for a recommendation that one of the five companies in the divisional machine-gun battalion "be equipped as a tank company." The proposal submitted by Pershing on September 23, 1917, was based on an AEF strength of 20 combat and 10 depot/replacement divisions. The schedule included 30 light tank companies with divisions and 30 with field army troops. An additional 15 companies of heavy tanks were allocated to the army troops. In the rear area 10 training and replacement companies and seven depot companies were provided for repair and salvage of tanks. The total personnel strength of the AEF Tank Corps, based on the 30 divisions, was 14,827. As with most plans, many changes ensued as the Tank Corps in France began to take shape.

At Camp Colt, Pennsylvania, near Gettysburg, the US Army had established a tank training center. Dwight Eisenhower served at Camp Colt until the end of the war, finishing as a lieutenant colonel. In addition to Camp Colt, armored training was conducted at four other sites, two in Pennsylvania and two in North Carolina. Most recruits destined to serve in the Tank Corps in France received their initial training at those facilities.

There was a shortage of tanks for training. Fewer than 1,000 light tanks on the Renault model were manufactured in the United States, but none participated in combat with the US Tank Corps—all the machines used by the Americans in France were of French and British manufacture. Looking to the future, the US Ordnance Department stationed an officer in France to facilitate the assembly of heavy tanks using

Brigadier General Samuel D. Rockenbach commanded the Tank Corps in the AEF from December 1917 until the Armistice. Prior to his return to the US in June 1919, he briefly commanded Base Section I of the SOS in St. Nazaire, France. Photo taken April 25, 1919, in his HQ. (US Signal Corps, 160132)

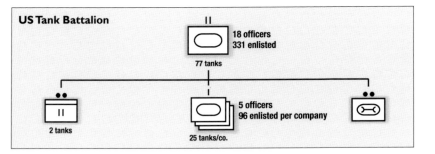

parts manufactured elsewhere. The Liberty engine developed for aircraft provided the power plant for the joint US-British designed heavy tank, the Mark VIII "Liberty." The story was the same as for the light tank—no tank of this design made it into action. There was bureaucratic friction between US manufacturers anxious to produce tanks and the AEF staff officers who were trying their best to procure tanks in France. Major James A. Drain served as the US representative on the Inter-allied Tank Commission "to coordinate production efforts." Additionally, the British and Americans had agreed in January 1918 to establish a factory to produce the Mark VIII tanks in France with a target of "fifteen hundred tanks during the year 1918."

When General Rockenbach arrived at Langres he found a very small but energetic staff. He directed the organization of a light tank school at Bourg, procured tanks from the French and began recruiting men for the crews. By the summer of 1918, when the American First Army was being organized during the Aisne–Marne counter-offensive in July and August, the Tank Corps was firmly established. Modifications in the organization to accommodate the increasing size of the AEF were reported to the War Department in August 1918. Tank troops would be part of the GHQ, AEF, and "belong to the strategical reserve" in sufficient numbers to support a group of field armies of 80 divisions scheduled to be on hand by mid-summer 1919. Two tank brigades, with all of the combat and combat support units necessary for operations, were planned so that two armies could be supported.

The energy of a few determined American tank officers had produced a mixed force of US crewed French Renaults supported by heavy tanks from the French army sufficient to provide combat assault vehicles for two army corps in the St. Mihiel operation that began on September 12, 1918. Patton had managed to organize two battalions of light tanks at the school at Bourg in time for the operation. Lt. Colonel Patton commanded the US 1st Tank Brigade and Lt. Colonel Daniel Pullen commanded the 3d Tank Brigade, which consisted only of his headquarters, but it was capable of providing coordination between the American and French tank units. It was patchwork organization, but adequate.

The story of the Tank Corps in the battle phases from mid-September through the Armistice on November 11 was one of improvisation, disciplined leadership and heroic field maintenance. Keeping enough tanks in action to make a difference in battle challenged Patton and his colleagues to the limit of their resources. The AEF Tank Corps made a significant contribution to American battle history.

The Services of Supply (SOS)

Field Service Regulations provided for a Line of Communications (LOC) organization "to relieve the combatant forces from every consideration except that of defeating the enemy." The LOC for the AEF gradually evolved into the robust supply, service, and transportation organization known as the Services of Supply (SOS) by March 13, 1918. Major General James Harbord, AEF chief-of-staff, noted that GHQ at Chaumont looked like a "deserted village" when the train pulled out to take the SOS staff to its new headquarters in Tours. With the division of the staff between GHQ at Chaumont and SOS at Tours, the AEF had begun the process of "growing" into a fully developed theater army organization. All technical staff departments went to Tours, but the Adjutant General, the Inspector General, and the Judge Advocate General, who provided command services, remained in Chaumont. Added were the chiefs of the Artillery and the Tank Corps. Geographically, the SOS included all of France and Great Britain but was divided into seven base sections, an intermediate section, an advance section and independent districts at Paris and Tours, the latter being the Headquarters.

Near the end of the war, several other base sections were established to accommodate forces in Italy and in 1919 for the occupation zone along the Rhine River. The SOS was a small army within an army.

This map shows the logistical organization of the Services of Supply (SOS) of the AEF. Previously known as the Line of Communications and the Service of the Rear, the SOS coordinated the transportation, supply and communication requirements of the AEF from its Headquarters at Tours. The numbers designate the seven (ultimately nine) base sections, the major subordinate units of the SOS. The AEF used the ports of Brest, St. Nazaire and several farther south, thus reserving the northern French ports for the British and French armies

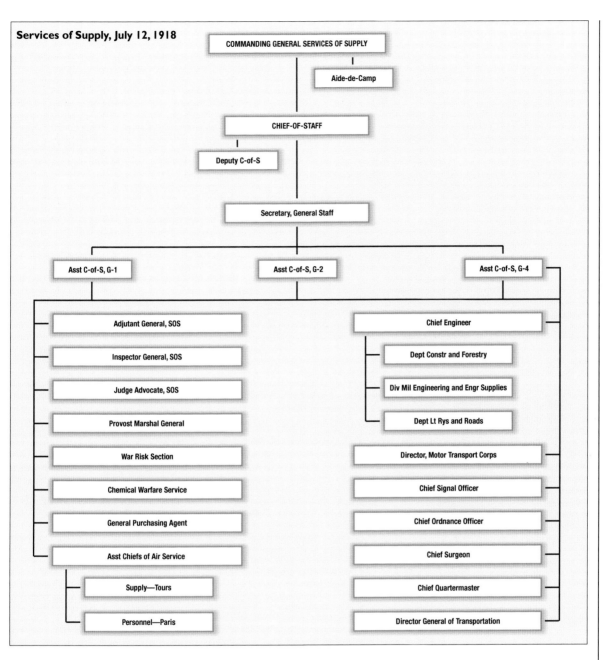

Services of Supply, July 12, 1918

- COMMANDING GENERAL SERVICES OF SUPPLY
  - Aide-de-Camp
- CHIEF-OF-STAFF
  - Deputy C-of-S
- Secretary, General Staff
- Asst C-of-S, G-1
- Asst C-of-S, G-2
- Asst C-of-S, G-4
  - Adjutant General, SOS
  - Inspector General, SOS
  - Judge Advocate, SOS
  - Provost Marshal General
  - War Risk Section
  - Chemical Warfare Service
  - General Purchasing Agent
  - Asst Chiefs of Air Service
    - Supply—Tours
    - Personnel—Paris
  - Chief Engineer
    - Dept Constr and Forestry
    - Div Mil Engineering and Engr Supplies
    - Dept Lt Rys and Roads
  - Director, Motor Transport Corps
  - Chief Signal Officer
  - Chief Ordnance Officer
  - Chief Surgeon
  - Chief Quartermaster
  - Director General of Transportation

On July 29, 1918, General Pershing appointed Harbord, his former chief-of-staff, then later commander of the 2d Division during the fighting in the Marne salient, to replace Major General Francis J. Kernan as the commanding general of the Services of Supply. Pershing took this decision to preserve his freedom of action and his command prerogatives in the AEF. The War Department had indicated that it was considering the assignment to France of Major General George W. Goethals, an engineer of considerable reputation who in retirement was directing supply activities for the army in Washington. The notion to place Goethals in charge of the SOS, which then would provide service to the AEF but report directly to the War Department, seems to have originated with General Peyton C. March, the army chief-of-staff. There was some intrigue and rumor accompanying the change of SOS command, but Secretary Baker and General Pershing handled the event professionally. Goethals did not come to France,

Major General Mason N. Patrick, former commander of the 1st Engineer Regiment. Appointed to succeed Brig. Gen. Benjamin D. Foulois as Chief of the Air Service on May 29, 1918. Promoted to major general on July 11, 1918. Pershing selected his West Point classmate to eliminate rivalries in the Air Service command structure. He was an engineer, not a flying officer, during the war. In the 1920s he again led the Air Service and learned to fly. (US Signal Corps, 73514)

other than to visit Pershing at Chaumont in early July 1918. Harbord, with his extensive staff experience and his brief division command understood the need for effective logistical operations if the AEF were to succeed. As supplies and services moved from the rear to the front a smooth handoff from SOS to the "G staff" of the AEF, GHQ, was essential. The St. Mihiel campaign was the first test of this logistical system. Lieutenant Colonel George C. Marshall has been given widespread credit for planning the complex operational transition from the St. Mihiel campaign to the Meuse–Argonne campaign in mid-September 1918, and rightfully so. But even George Marshall could not have accomplished that feat without the smooth functioning logistical organization under the command of James Harbord.

The engineers

Fighting on top of the earth required shelter under the nap of the earth so that troops about to engage in close action would be protected from direct and indirect fires as well as the ever-present possibility of attacks with chemical weapons—gas and flame. In order to provide protection, engineers prepared elaborate systems of trenches of both the fighting variety and also communications pathways. All of this earth moving and the associated trades such as mining and quarrying fell to a hardy group of soldiers called engineers in the American service. The heavy demand of trench warfare required units specifically charged to prepare gun emplacements and underground shelters, in addition to the more common tasks of road and bridge repair in the combat zone. Regiments of pioneer infantry were organized to provide this service. The pioneer infantrymen were less skilled than engineer soldiers. The other major armies in France used these types of soldiers to augment the engineer units. In the AEF, the pioneer infantry regiments were assigned to corps and armies. African-American soldiers manned about half of the 37 regiments raised for service in France.

Each combat division had a regiment of engineers that was organic, meaning standard, to the organization. In addition to the field engineering tasks, the American engineers built port facilities, developed large-scale lumbering operations to feed the demand for construction timber, and built both standard and narrow-gauge railways. The 11th Engineer Regiment soldiers served in the British zone of operations and were among the first Americans in combat in France. Behind the lines the engineers built the depots and covered storage needed to supply the rapidly expanding combat units of the AEF. The

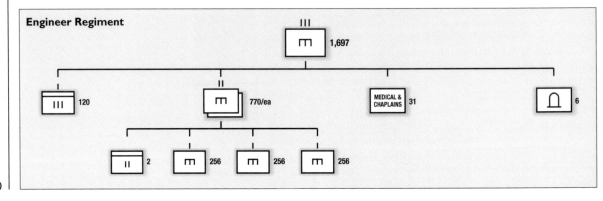

AEF Engineer Regiments (Based on TO&E of June 26, 1918)		
Personnel		
Unit/Section	**26 Jun 1918**	**Strength**
Regimental HQ & HQ Co.	1	120
Engineer Battalions	2	770 ea
Battalion HQ	2	2 ea
Engineer Company	6	256 ea
Total Combatants	–	**1,660**
Medical Dept. & Chaplains	–	31
Ordnance Dept.	–	6
Regiment Aggregate	1	**1,697**
Animals		
Draft Horses	–	108
Riding Horses	–	94
Draft Mules	–	104
Pack Mules	–	48
Total Horses and Mules	–	**354**
Major Equipment Items		
Rolling Kitchens (4-mule)	–	7
Water Carts (1-mule)	–	6
Medical Carts (1-mule)	–	2
Ration & Baggage Carts (2-mule)	–	6
Combat Tool Wagons (4-horse)	–	24
Combat Tool Wagons (4-mule)	–	6
Ration & Baggage Wagons (4-mule)	–	7
Bicycles	–	24
Motor Cars	–	1
Motorcycles with Sidecar	–	16
Pistols	–	179
Rifles	–	1,487

Source: United States Army In The World War 1917–1919. Volume 1: Organization of the American Expeditionary Forces *(Washington: Historical Division, Department of the Army, 1948)*

air parks (airfields), barracks, food storage facilities, and mapping needed to keep the two million soldiers of the AEF in action were all provided by the engineers. Often the impact of logistics on combat operations is overlooked, but in World War I it was quite evident. The secondary mission of engineer units is to fight as infantry when circumstances required. During the reduction of the Aisne–Marne salient in July and August 1918, the 2d Division's engineers fought bravely and took significant casualties. In the fighting between the Meuse River and the Argonne Forest in October 1918, Sergeant Wilbur Colyer of the 1st Engineer Regiment attacked German machine-gun emplacements and was awarded the Medal of Honor, one of five received by 1st Division soldiers in World War I. That medal is on display in the 1st Division Museum at Cantigny in Wheaton, Illinois.

ABOVE Major General Hunter Liggett reviews First Army's "famous colored band" at Vadney, north of Chalons, December 18, 1918. (US Signal Corps, 49570)

Black American soldiers volunteered for service in France in large numbers, many more than the US War Department was willing to induct. Two divisions, the 92d and the 93d, were organized in 1917. The 92d "Buffalo" Division was established on October 24, 1917, with inductees from all over the nation making up the units. General and field officers, plus officers above the grade of 1st lieutenant in the technical branches and the artillery were white. On October 26, Brevet Major General Charles C. Ballou, West Point classmate of John Pershing, took command of the 92d at Camp Upton, Long Island. He had been the commanding officer of the Colored Officers Training Camp at Des Moines, Iowa, but his own attitude was that African-American soldiers should not be in combat. He was finally removed from his post near the end of the war, and reverted to the rank of colonel after demobilization of the AEF. The 92d comprised the 183d and 184th Infantry Brigades, and the 167th Field Artillery Brigade, was assigned to Liggett's I Corps during the Meuse–Argonne campaign.

The 93d division, although established on November 23, 1917, with the 185th and 186th Infantry Brigades of African-American soldiers, but no artillery brigade, never served in combat as a division. The four regiments of the division, 369th, 370th, 371st, and 372d, had been brought into federal service from the National Guard and served under the provisional command of Brigadier General Roy Hoffman until May 15, 1918, when three of the regiments were placed under the operational control of the Fourth French Army. They were reorganized to conform to the French infantry organization. The 370th Infantry Regiment was assigned to the Seventh French Army.

Medical services

Medicine and nursing with the AEF were extensions of the War Department Staff. Like engineering and other technical branches of the army, medical services were both an organizational responsibility and a "stove-pipe" vertical structure of technical services. The responsibility of providing medical and nursing services to the AEF was shared by the GHQ staff and the SOS. As arrivals of American troops in the summer of 1918 surged, there was a shortage of adequate medical staff and facilities. The health of the AEF was, according to Harbord, "remarkably good" considering the incidence of diphtheria, measles, mumps, diarrhea, influenza, and pneumonia as causes leading to non-effective soldiers. Influenza and accompanying pneumonia were a more serious problem for the army in the United States than in the AEF by a factor of ten to one. Venereal disease, due to the personal intervention of Pershing in setting priorities for his Surgeon General, was significantly lower than was common in large armies. By the time the influenza epidemic peaked in October 1918, simultaneously with the increase in casualties from the Meuse–Argonne campaign, hospital beds were more than sufficient to meet the demand. General Harbord credited the fleets of light ambulances serving the front areas and the creation of large hospital centers, such as those in the vicinity of Toul, as two significant advances in medical support to the army.

American Expeditionary Forces, North Russia; American Expeditionary Forces Siberia; American Forces in France; American Forces in Germany

These organizations were created to provide command, control, and support to forces operating in Russia and forces conducting the occupation in France and Germany during the post-hostilities period of demobilization.

Tactics

In the 19th century, tactics for the United States Army was synonymous with parade-ground drill. Drill was governed for units of regimental size and smaller by a series of manuals, usually adapted from the French versions. *Infantry Drill Regulations 1911* was in use, with minor updates, in 1917 as the United States prepared to send forces to France.

Doctrine for brigades and divisions was communicated by *Field Service Regulations*. The edition of 1914, updated frequently throughout the war, provided the guidance from the War Department to the field units.

General Pershing had a specific idea as to how his AEF should fight in France. The French, and to a lesser degree the British, believed that fighting from trenches using close-combat weapons, notably the bayonet, trench mortars, and grenades, was the most effective tactic derived from several years of fighting the Germans on the Western Front. The objective of trench fighting was to attack and seize the enemy's trenches. The American Army, said Pershing, should fight in "open warfare" style, that is with scouts in the van, irregular formations and timetables, reliance on the fire of infantry weapons in the assault, the use of terrain features and cover, brief orders and a reliance on the initiative of individual soldiers to outmaneuver and defeat the enemy. Allied soldiers were trained to fight from the trenches that had spread from the English Channel to the Swiss frontier once the war of movement in 1914 had spent itself. Using the tools of miners to burrow into the earth and the weapons of close combat, such as clubs, knives, and hand grenades, the infantry scurried from shell hole to shell hole across the ruptured earth of no man's land to grapple with their enemy. It was not the war of movement that the American commander-in-chief had visualized.

While Pershing was arguing with his War Department that doughboys training in the US be trained to fire their rifles accurately up to 600 yards, French army trainers who had been sent to prepare American soldiers for warfare "taught trench, not open, warfare, and the War Department deferred to their experience." There is scant evidence of "open warfare" in US doctrinal records. Although the concept seemed logical and Pershing and his AEF staff often referred to it in training literature and critiques of training, neither *Field*

Pershing and A.E.F. Generals, World War I, 1923–25, artist G. B. Matthews, oil on canvas, 118 by 216in., US Army Art Collection. (Permission of US Army Center of Military History for use of image)

Major General George W. Read, commander of II Corps, comprising the 27th and 30th Divisions. Photo taken on October 5, 1918, at Assevillers, France, on the Somme River. The corps headquarters was at Ham. (US Signal Corps, 26488)

Service Regulations nor tactical manuals had much to say about the details of how open warfare was to be conducted at the maneuver unit, i.e. regiment and brigade level. This concept of fighting was not effectively communicated to those who had to execute it in battle—the junior officers, noncommissioned officers, and soldiers. Robert Bullard, who commanded units from regiment through field army, explained that every "war of consequence brings its new things in training and methods" and World War I was no exception. But, "before our declaration of war," he said, "the determined pacifism of our government had effectually prevented any study by our army of these changes." Bullard, writing in 1925, criticized the Allied high command for not recognizing that trench warfare was a step in the process toward open warfare, not an end in itself. He said that the American trainers stuck to their guns and the "correctness of their view" that "offense, open warfare, became the guiding principle of American training in France." It is not surprising that Bullard resonated the Pershing philosophy of training and fighting because Pershing had moved Bullard from command of a brigade in the 1st Division shortly after arrival in France and made him chief of AEF schools.

Lieutenant General Hunter Liggett wrote in 1928 that very shortly after his arrival in France, Pershing "made up his mind to a number of things." Among these precepts were (1) the immediate need for one million doughboys, and ultimately three million; (2) the mission of the AEF must be offensive, not defensive; that training would be "primarily in offensive tactics and open warfare ... that the war would be decided in the open;" (3) the American Army would not be amalgamated; it would fight in its own sector under its own officers. In an earlier book, General Liggett explained his introduction to the Western Front and British and French training methods in the fall of 1917. Because his division, the 41st, was en route to France, Liggett remained at Chaumont after his observation assignment in the British sector. By mid-January he was in command of I Corps, newly organized at Neufchâteau. But even Liggett, of whom Pershing had spoken critically early in the war, seemed convinced that the American Army in France was training correctly and effectively "under open warfare conditions."

These doctrinal differences in tactical performance were more than illusory. On May 1, 1918, General Henri Pétain, French commander of the Armies of the North and Northeast, issued a long memo on training the Americans.

It noted that "American units arriving in France have only had, up to the present, very incomplete instructions," which were limited to "gymnastic exercises, close-order drill, rifle fire and drill in field warfare, which consisted too much of small operations, having but little relation to actual warfare." He went on to say that "Americans dream of operating in open country, after having broken through the front. This results in too much attention being devoted to this form of operations, which the Americans consider as superior, and in which, our Allies sometimes seem to think, we are incapable of offering them the same assistance which they expect from us in trench warfare." He ordered his armies "To take discreet measures to counteract the idea that we are inexperienced in open warfare" and "To direct into proper channels ... the excellent leaning toward open warfare, and to instruct them on this subject for the purpose of instilling an understanding of mass warfare." Pétain concluded with the wise observation that "The main purpose of our collaboration in the instruction of American troops is to give our Allies the benefit of our dearly bought experience ... Constant patience and extreme tact, together with application will serve to overcome all obstacles."

But the actual result of this training approach was that the Americans fought in their early engagements from May into August 1918 at Cantigny, Belleau Wood, along the Marne, and south of Soissons, just as they had been trained by the French, with straight-ahead assaults supported by plenty of artillery and mortar fire. The attendant casualties were staggering. Part of the explanation for this unhappy result is that American divisions were fighting as part of French corps and field armies and therefore subject to French doctrine in battle formations, except in the British sector where the 27th and 30th Divisions were controlled by II Corps. Those two divisions had trained with the British, along with eight others that were subsequently reassigned to the AEF.

Another part of the answer lies in the incompleteness of the training of American divisions. The 1st Division was the only one to complete its three-phase cycle of battle preparation. All the others had something less. Finally, the demands of terrain and the actions of the Germans in many instances precluded any approach other than straight-ahead fighting; there were no flanks—strategic, operational or tactical—on the Western Front, except those made by a penetration of the enemy lines or an irregular advance of fighting units in the attack. As Timothy Nenninger noted in a recent article in the *Journal of Military History*, "The term 'doctrine' was not used much in the US Army during World War I." When we remember that the United States had been a belligerent for only 19 months and the AEF had been a participant in active combat operations for only five months at the time of the Armistice, it is remarkable that any tactical coherence was achieved, not that it was inadequate.

Infantry companies, battalions, and regiments supported by machine guns, mortars, and artillery, carried the burden of the fighting. Tanks, airplanes, and additional artillery made the battlefield a grisly arena with the terrain ruptured by the continual bombardment and laced with poison gas. The barbed-wire entanglements, emplaced by both Allies and Germans, slowed movement through no man's land and thereby presented vulnerable targets for the machine guns and rifles on both sides. As Allan Millett noted in his study of the Cantigny battle at the end of May 1918, the German Army had not yet perfected its offensive infiltration tactics, but "it had already developed a system of flexible defense that confounded the Allies." The German defensive positions were constructed in great depth, lightly held by strongpoints strengthened by machine guns in the forward area, and increasingly resilient in the main battle area. For a German regiment, only one of its battalions occupied the forward positions and the main battle area, which was about 1km wide and perhaps 2km deep. The other battalions had missions of support (counterattack) and reserve well outside the range of Allied artillery. This flexible organization of the enemy defenses left few attack options to the American infantry.

Major General Beaumont B. Buck. General Buck commanded the 2d Infantry Brigade, 1st Division, as a brigadier (one-star) general during the Cantigny and Soissons operations. On August 27, 1918, he took command of the 3d Division until he was relieved by General Pershing during the Meuse–Argonne campaign in mid-October 1918. (US Signal Corps, 24372)

Cantigny: a regimental attack supported by the division

The German spring offensives of 1918 presented a crisis for the Allies. Marshal Ferdinand Foch was chosen at Doullens on March 26 to coordinate Allied strategy, and at Beauvais on April 3 the governments of Great Britain, France, and the United States charged him with "the strategic direction of military operations." Pershing immediately made available his four combat-ready divisions. The first place chosen was in Picardy near the farming village of Cantigny. On April 25 the 1st Division made the first appearance of American fighters in a combat action.

When the 1st attacked and seized the heights and the village of Cantigny "with splendid dash" on May 28, Pershing was among the group of observers. "The desperate efforts of the Germans," said Pershing "gave the fighting at Cantigny a seeming tactical importance entirely out of proportion to the numbers involved." Lieutenant Colonel George C. Marshall, the division operations officer, understood that the attack was of "limited objective" and as such the 28th Infantry Regiment would not penetrate far enough beyond Cantigny to take the German artillery out of action. This was to be a regimental attack conducted by the entire division. Marshall, and Brigadier General Charles P. Summerall, commander of the 1st Artillery Brigade, planned the entire

Lieutenant Colonel Clarence Ralph Huebner, commander in succession G Company, 2d Battalion, 28th Infantry Regiment, then the battalion and the regiment as casualties produced vacancies. Huebner entered the army as a private and was promoted quickly due to competence. (MRC)

operation. Brigadier General Beaumont P. Buck, commander of the 2d Infantry Brigade, and Colonel Hanson E. Ely, commander of the 28th Infantry Regiment, who were the maneuver unit commanders for the upcoming battle, were responsible for preparing their soldiers for the fight, but had little input to the design of the attack.

The 28th rehearsed the attack on May 24 on similar ground about 12 miles to the rear. Twelve French Schneider tanks and "a section of flame fighters were assigned to the regiment." Ely's troops rehearsed for two days while the 18th Infantry Regiment relieved them in the line and completed work on the forward trenches. As the day of attack approached, that fickle attendant of all battles, chance, intervened. A detachment led by an engineer lieutenant was moving heavy entrenching tools forward to the jump-off trenches during the dark night of May 26. The group stumbled into the German trenches. After taking fire from the Germans, and from their own front lines, the group was led back by the infantry officer accompanying the 50 men. However, the engineer lieutenant was missing, along with his map that probably revealed the location of the American trenches and supply dumps. If that was not enough, the sacks of entrenching tools left behind probably made the German intelligence officer's task easy. The afternoon of that same day, Lieutenant Colonel Marshall's horse slipped and fell on him with his left ankle "remaining in the stirrup and sustaining [a] painful fracture." The doctor taped it up and the operations chief continued with his duties—for about a week! After the Armistice, the body of the lost engineer was discovered in a grave north of Cantigny.

The entire regiment was put into the assault line, with only one company in reserve. Marshall designated two companies of the 18th Infantry Regiment as a reserve for the 2d Infantry Brigade because the other regiment of that brigade—the 26th—was fully committed in another sector of the battlefield. Support from French corps and army artillery tripled the number of guns available for the assault.

Two participants in the battle, Captain Clarence R. Huebner, commander of G Company and later commander of the 2d Battalion, 28th Infantry Regiment, and Colonel Ely, the regimental commander, each reported on the results of the capture of Cantigny. Huebner had succeeded to battalion command when Lieutenant Colonel Robert J. Maxey was mortally wounded. The battalion occupied the center of the regimental attack formation, with each company in the battalion disposed with two platoons in the first line of two waves separated by 20 yards, and, 150 yards to the rear, two platoons in the second line, also of two waves. There was one machine gun on each flank of the second line of the company, and the support company was positioned farther to the rear. During the night, Huebner related in his report on June 2, the battalion was in position at half past midnight but could not move until 0330hrs because German artillery fires had blown up the regimental dump, thereby delaying the movement of supplies forward. The battalion attacked with the regiment at 0645hrs "and encountered very little resistance until CANTIGNY was passed and [the] enemy's second position" was taken. After a short, sharp fight the battalion dug in and emplaced barbed wire, which was brought forward by the fifth (training and replacement) platoons of each company. The first German counterattack came about noon and a second at about 1900hrs on May 28. The enemy never reached the battalion wire during the several attacks over the next three days. During the night of May 29–30, water, food, and other supplies were brought forward. "Discipline during the entire engagement," Huebner reported, "was excellent as a whole. In a few isolated cases a few men were hard to control, but this was quickly overcome." The battalion lost five officers and 75 enlisted men killed, six officers and 179 enlisted men wounded, and one officer and six enlisted men missing, mostly "to artillery fire after consolidation, and to machine-gun fire during consolidation."

In his after-action report, Major George F. Rozelle, Jr., who commanded the 28th Infantry's 1st Battalion on the right of the regimental attack line, noted that "It was also reported that the enemy at first seemed to expose himself in a reckless manner about 200 meters in front of Battalion A [1-28 Inf.], and we were led to believe that he was unaccustomed to receiving effective rifle fire at that range. A/2 [B-1-28 Inf.] and A/3 [D-1-28 Inf.] reported that our rifle fire was very effective at that range and caused the enemy many casualties." Lieutenant Colonel J. M. Cullison, commanding the 3d Battalion of the 28th on the far left of the regimental line, reported that the attack on Cantigny went forward promptly without confusion because "every detail had been worked out, and possible contingencies foreseen." However, the goblin of uncertainty struck the battalion while it was consolidating its objective line on the north side of the village. A specious order to withdraw to "our front trench line" caused the men of L and K Companies on the left of the battalion line to withdraw "in an orderly manner by echelon." Cullison reacted quickly by ordering his own I Company and G Company of the 18th Infantry that was in reserve to reoccupy the vacated positions. Had the Germans reacted quickly against the 3d Battalion, which was without its trench mortars and 37mm guns, Cullison did not have the fire support necessary to retake the positions. M Company had held fast and allowed the battalion to recover from its mistake. As a result, the regimental commander, Ely, ordered that false withdrawal orders were to be dealt with swiftly and severely, even if it was necessary to fire on their own troops to prevent the movement to the rear.

Colonel Ely filed a very detailed report of the attack on Cantigny. He noted that the infantry units had been "brought up in trucks" and unloaded at about 2300hrs on May 27. They proceeded forward along "routes previously reconnoitered, avoiding shelled areas." After the objective line was taken, patrols and automatic rifles were pushed forward "to cover the consolidation." The "rolling barrage was extremely accurate, enabling the infantry to follow at less than 50 yards." Within 90 minutes of seizing the objective "the line of resistance was practically continuous" with entrenched soldiers and wire. Three strongpoints were established by the third wave as soon as it closed the objective line. Each strongpoint consisted of "a platoon of infantry with two US auto. rifles, four machine guns and one captured German machine gun. Trenches were built in form of cross to face in any direction."

The divisional engineers and the attached French tanks and flamethrower unit were very effective. Regarding the rehearsal before the battle, Ely said, "If a longer period could have been used for this preliminary preparation a few rough edges could have been better smoothed off." Concerning casualties he said, "Each time the counter-battery [artillery] work ceased, heavy losses began." During the first counterattack at about 1200hrs on May 28, eight German airplanes strafed the American positions from about 300 to 600 yards altitude, "firing into our lines and correcting the artillery until they had the exact range." About one-third of the regiment's casualties were from enemy machine-gun fire and the rest from artillery. A certain measure of tactical surprise had been achieved because the Germans believed that the artillery fires that preceded the infantry attack were simply a fire raid on their lines in retaliation for a German raid on the night of May 26–27. "The attack was a complete surprise, and close following of the barrage by our troops enabled them to capture and clean up all enemy troops in CANTIGNY with almost no losses." Based on intelligence and operations reports, Ely said that total German casualties were "from 1,900 to 2,200" not including casualties far in the enemy rear caused by friendly artillery.

The 1st Division's artillery brigade commander was experienced in the organization of artillery for combat, having served in China at the turn of the century and later in the Philippines where he distinguished himself repeatedly. But the difference at Cantigny was that this was a battle that required the integration of the fires of the three artillery regiments and the

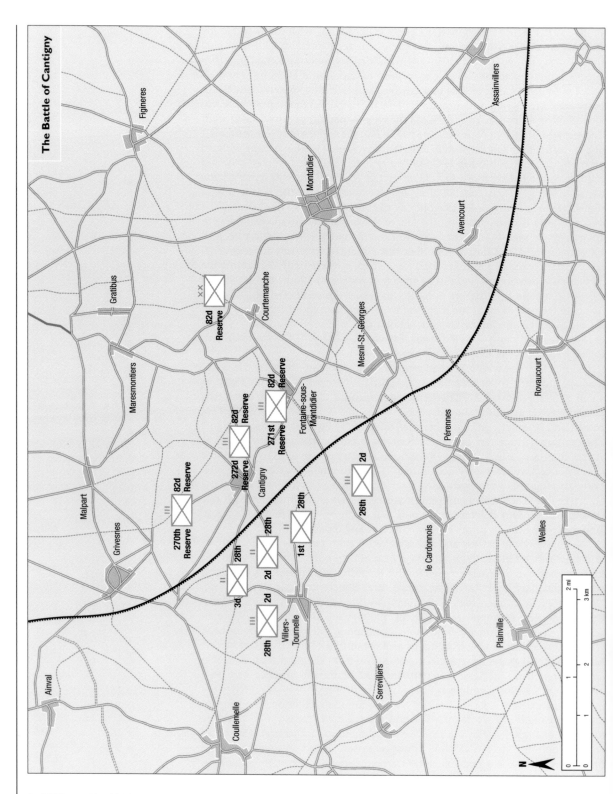

At 0645hrs on May 28, 1918, the 28th Infantry Regiment, 1st Division, attacked two German regiments holding the Montdidier salient outside of Cantigny. The regiment attacked with three battalions on the line that were accompanied by tanks and flamethrowers. Cantigny was in American hands in the morning, but the Germans counterattacked twice during the afternoon and were repulsed each time. The fighting continued for two more days when the 28th Infantry was relieved by another regiment of the 1st Division, the 16th Infantry.

trench mortar battalion "organic" to the division with the supporting fires from French units at corps and army level. The degree of sophistication required of General Summerall and his staff challenged their collective experiences.

How did artillery regiments conduct the fire-support battle? The 5th Field Artillery, equipped with French Schneider 155mm howitzers, along with the supporting French artillery units, provided the pre-attack concentrations and destructive fires targeted on known German positions and locations like crossroads where the flow of reinforcements could be impeded. This was accomplished by detailed fire planning that

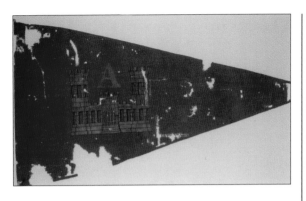

Guidon of A Company, 1st Engineer Regiment. The guidon was carried in battle at Cantigny on May 28–31, 1918, and shows the damage, probably from hostile fire. (FDM)

was time-phased to the anticipated progress of the infantry assault. Map overlays were prepared so that the infantry and supporting unit commanders would know what to expect. Cantigny was a fairly simple, straightforward attack but the potential for mistakes in the coordination of fires and the ground assault was significant. Also, the command and control measures available to make adjustments to fire during the battle were not flexible or even reliable. 2d Lieutenant E. E. Hills, a 5th Field Artillery liaison officer with the 26th Infantry Regiment on May 27, 1918, during a German raid, noted:

> To my mind the weak link exists from the front line to the Inf. Bn. The reports [that] came in at the time of the operation were greatly exaggerated due to undue excitement. A minute detailed report from the Infantry has never been made to my knowledge. I feel that the forward organizations should be required to render an exact report when barrages or fires are called for and more information should be given in regard to the particular operation involved. The Infantry Commander arranged for this at one time but compliance is not evident. In the past it has been hard for the artillery liaison officer to render complete, intelligent reports due to lack of information from front line commanders.

At the battalion and company level very basic means such as colored flares were used to start, shift, and stop supporting fires. On one occasion the pyrotechnic signals used by the front-line infantry to shift fires from a French battery were compromised when an American soldier deserted. This soldier knew the pyrotechnic signal codes for "barrage," "lengthen fire," and "gas." When the American infantry subsequently used those signals, the Germans immediately replied with the same flare signals in an effort to cause erratic firing. The lesson, of course, was frequent changing of the pyrotechnic signal codes. The AEF depended almost exclusively on wire, meaning telephones, to transmit information between the infantry and the artillery, although the wire was frequently broken by shellfire. Wireless communications, meaning radios, did exist but were bulky and heavy. However, the battalion commander of the 1st Battalion, 6th Field Artillery, Lieutenant Colonel John W. Downer, did conclude in his report to his regimental commander on June 2, 1918, that "the best means of communication are (1) Wireless (2) Runners (3) Rockets. No difficulties of liaison were encountered during the attack."

The other two regiments, the 6th and 7th Field Artillery, were equipped with French Schneider 75mm light artillery pieces. The 75mm was a rapid-firing gun suitable for laying down the rolling barrages. 1st Lieutenant Wm. O. Coleman, liaison officer from the 6th Field Artillery to the 18th Infantry Regiment, recommended in his report of June 1, 1918, that "the T.P.S. and the T.F.S. [variations of the ground-return telephone and telegraph systems] be used more than heretofore and that at the same time the telephones be kept running, with a double line to all posts of importance."

Pershing did not have the time he needed to train the AEF units in a progressive and orderly manner. Professionalism required for effective infantry–artillery cooperation was lacking. During the postwar period work on centralized fire direction and control methods, to include forward observation using radio, was one of the lessons of combat in World War I.

"The heights of Cantigny were of no strategic importance, and of small tactical value," said George Marshall. "The issue was a moral one." Had the Americans been visibly and roundly defeated at Cantigny, the Germans as well as the other Allies would have concluded that the doughboys were not up to the task. But the attack was successful, as were the three days of defense that followed. "We held Cantigny. The Germans never afterwards reoccupied the village."

Soissons: a divisional attack as part of a French corps

Major General Charles P. Summerall, promoted from his post of divisional artillery brigade commander, commanded the 1st Division from July 15 to October 12, 1918, when he took over the V Corps. His major operations were the Aisne–Marne campaign (Soissons) and the short St. Mihiel attack in mid-September.

Summerall took command of the 1st Division three days prior to its attack in the Soissons operation. He was quite familiar with the division, its staff, and its brigade and regimental commanders. The movement from the Cantigny–Montdidier sector to the west of Soissons was arduous. Torrential rain fell on the night of July 17, clogging the limited road network for the approach march. The division was assigned to the XX (French) Corps (Berdoulat), part of the Tenth French Army (Mangin), along with the 2d (US) [Harbord] and 1st Moroccan (Daugan) Divisions for the attack from west to east against the west face of the German salient. The salient, created as part of the great German attacks of the spring of 1918, stretched from Soissons to Reims along the Aisne and Vesle rivers at its shoulders, and south to Château-Thierry at its nose.

Major Joseph Dorst Patch was transferred from the 26th Infantry Regiment to take command of the 1st Battalion, 18th Infantry Regiment, in early May 1918. His battalion had been in reserve at Roquencourt during the Cantigny fight where he discovered that he had "really inherited a fine battalion." By the time of the Soissons attack, Patch was an experienced battalion commander in the regiment commanded by Colonel Frank Parker.

The 1st Division was the left unit of the XX Corps, the Moroccans were in the center and the 2d Division was on the right. The division had both infantry brigades up on line, the 2d Brigade (Brig. Gen. Buck) in the north, or left, and the 1st Brigade (Brig. Gen. Hines) in the south, or right.

The four infantry regiments were aligned from north to south: 28th, 26th, 16th, and 18th. The division's mission was to fight to the east and cut the Soissons to Paris road and railroad, which lay about 9km away. It took four days of hard fighting to get there. The 18th had moved forward to the eastern edge of the Compiègne Forest to a bivouac site near Longavesne using French lorries. Patch was provided with a motorcycle with a side seat and driver so that he could reconnoiter the approach route. The jump-off point was about 1km east of the village of Laversine. The 1st Brigade PC (post of command) was located in a large cave near Coeuvres and Colonel Parker's 18th Infantry Regiment PC was in another cave on the eastern side of Coeuvres. Patch and his company commanders spent July 17 making a reconnaissance of their zone of action. He had the help of French guides and was able to meet the commander of the French Foreign Legion battalion that was to be on his battalion's right.

The march to the line of departure on the night of July 17 was a nightmare. The roads were congested with "every kind of man, animal, and vehicle

Colonel Frank Parker, commander, 18th Infantry Regiment, in front of his PC (post of command), January 1918. During the latter stage of the Meuse–Argonne campaign, Parker commanded the 1st Division when it marched across the front of several other American divisions in an attempt to seize the city of Sedan. (US Signal Corps, 6129)

struggling to get through." Torrential rain broke just as the march had begun, but the battalion reached the 18th PC cave by 0100hrs on July 18, two hours late. The French guides were not the same men who had assisted with the reconnaissance; none had ever been forward of the PC! The night was so dark that soldiers had to put their hands on the shoulders of those in front of them to keep from breaking the column as the battalion moved forward toward the line of departure, arriving at about 0300hrs. The attack was scheduled for 0435hrs, but Patch still had not received his attack order from regimental HQ. The attack order arrived by runner at 0345hrs, all 17 paragraphs of it. Patch had already briefed his company commanders with the sketchy information he had at hand and sent them back to their companies, barely escaping a German artillery concentration that fell on the battalion's position. The 1st Division's barrage landed just to the front of the battalion right on schedule. "The shells screaming above us was sweet music, and off we started." Patch had appointed the battalion intelligence officer, 1st Lieutenant John R. Graham, to be the guide as the battalion moved forward. He had runners from each of the companies who were to be used to send information rearward. Graham was killed by machine-gun fire in the wheat fields during the advance. Patch's battalion advanced with A and B Companies in the van and C and D Companies following in reserve. Each company typically would deploy two platoons forward on a front of about 100m, with skirmishers to the front. The other two platoons, also abreast, would be about 100m to the rear. The company commander would be in the interval between the front and rear platoons, with his runners.

Portrait of Major General Charles P. Summerall from a family album in the collections of the McCormick Research Center in Wheaton, Illinois. Summerall went to France as a member of the Baker Board, then joined the 1st Division as commander of the artillery brigade. On July 18, 1918, he took command of the 1st Division at the outset of the Soissons campaign. (MRC)

The machine-gun company followed the battalion. It consisted of three platoons, each with four squads. Each of the 12 squads manned one machine gun. The rolling barrage advanced in front of the battalion at the rate of 100m every two minutes till it reached the first objective line 2km away along the road that ran northeast from the village of Dommiers. There the barrage paused for 20 minutes, then advanced at the same rate to the second objective, a line between Cravançon Farm to the eastern edge of the Missy-aux-Bois ravine. The barrage again halted for 40 minutes, then advanced at 100m per four minutes to the third and final objective for the first day's attack, a north to south line 500m east of the village of Chaudun. The pauses were to allow the troops to close up on the objective lines, reorganize a bit, and then continue the attack. The doughboys reached the first objective line on schedule at 0530hrs and continued the attack. German machine guns and artillery increased their fire, carving large swathes in the American infantry formations. Just before the third objective line had been reached, Patch realized that the 16th Infantry on the left and the French on the right were far behind his own battalion. Fire was pouring into his position from both flanks. At that moment he was wounded and unable to command. "Therefore, I was only in our biggest battle for about four hours." Command passed to Captain Albert Nathness of A Company, but he too was wounded a short time later. The 18th Regiment secured Chaudun after some hand-to-hand fighting. German airplanes had been active all day on July 18, bombing and machine-gunning the advancing doughboys. The batteries of the 1st Division's 6th and 7th Field Artillery Regiments (four French 75mm guns per battery) leap-frogged forward to extend their firing range throughout the day. The 1st Division had advanced about 6km that first day of the offensive. The Germans quickly reinforced the area, fearing that their advanced positions in the nose of the salient to the south were in danger of being cut off by the Allied attack south of Soissons. The ease with which the Americans had advanced at Cantigny in late May 1918 compared with the difficulties they experienced in the Soissons campaign is representative of the "on-the-job training" that all American divisions experienced in combat up to August 1918.

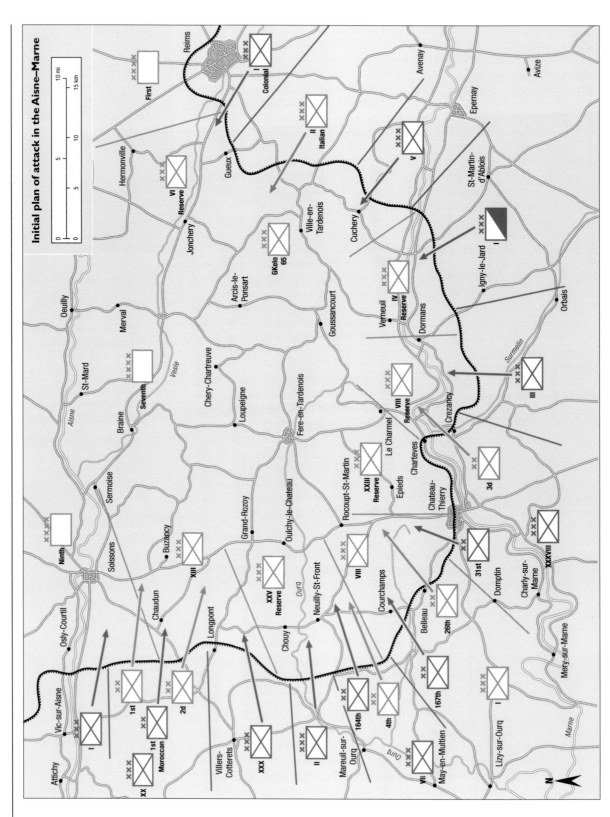

Initial plan of attack in the Aisne–Marne

In response to a projected major German offensive the Allies launched an attack to reduce the Aisne–Marne salient with the 1st and 2d American Divisions joining the 1st Moroccan Division in the French XX Corps to make an attack from west to east, south of Soissons.

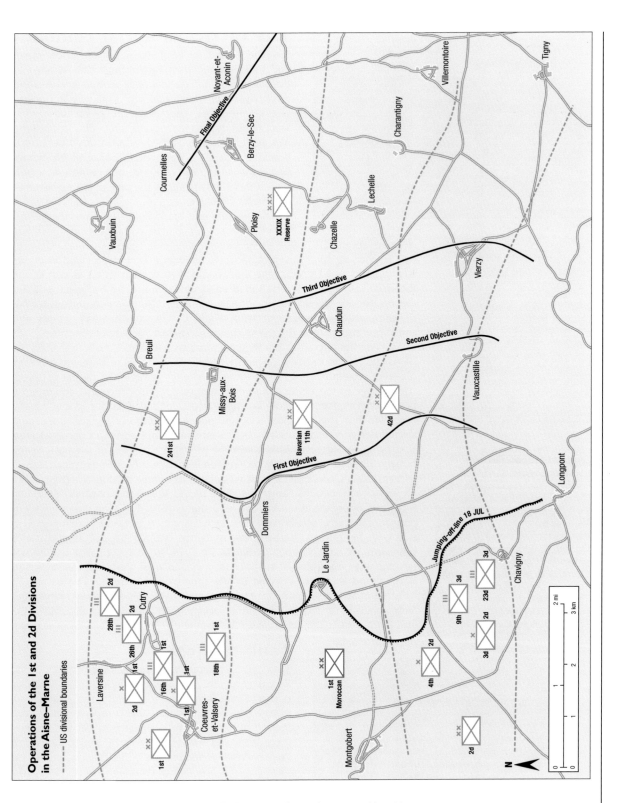

Operations of the 1st and 2d Divisions in the Aisne–Marne

- - - US divisional boundaries

On July 18, the 1st Division in the north and the 2d Division in the south, supported by a Moroccan division, attacked between Soissons and Château-Thierry. Although fighting was fierce and casualties were high, the Americans took 3,800 German prisoners and cut the Soissons–Château-Thierry road and seized the heights of Buzancy. The Germans then abandoned their Marne salient and retired to defensive positions at the Vesle River.

1st Division PC in a cave near Coeuvres during the Soissons campaign. The zone of advance of the American divisions was covered with caves and ravines, which the Germans effectively defended. (MRC)

Grave of Lieutenant Quentin Roosevelt, youngest son of President Theodore Roosevelt, near Chamery west of Reims. Roosevelt, a member of the 95th Aero Squadron based near Paris, was shot down by the Germans on Bastille Day, July 14, 1918. Following the gentlemen's code of the time, the German pilot landed and scratched Roosevelt's name on the propeller. The reputed engine cowling and propeller are on display in Château-Thierry. (US Signal Corps, 18907)

The tactics of aerial combat

Like the ground forces of the AEF, aviation personnel and units learned their tactics from the French and British. Initially the combat tasks were observation and reconnaissance, which gradually gave way to one-on-one aerial combat. The aviation units trained as they would fight, just as the ground forces did. In 1918 the Air Service of the AEF developed an operational bombing capability. The strength of the US Air Service had increased to nearly 200,000 officers and men with several thousand aircraft by the time of the Armistice in November 1918.

The pursuit (or fighter) pilot of 1918 was the knight, the airplane was his charger, and combat in the air was close and personal. Unlike their balloon-riding colleagues, American pilots of heavier-than-air craft wore no parachutes. Gradually successful air combat tactics were learned and refined. Americans began their combat flying as part of the Escadrille Lafayette (Lafayette Squadron), a unit commanded by French aviation officers. Ninety American flying officers transferred from French units in the fall of 1917, among them men who would command American groups and squadrons and instruct the newly commissioned US Air Service pilots.

Turning the aircraft into a weapon was a technological challenge. Both the Lewis and Hotchkiss machine guns were adapted to aerial warfare, but from the observer's cockpit behind the pilot or on the top wing. Aligning the gun with the fuselage of the plane required some means to fire "through" the rotating propeller. The French pilot, Roland Garros, devised deflector plates for the propeller, but this solution was not practical. Anthony Fokker, the Dutch aircraft designer, introduced in 1915 a gun synchronized with the propeller so that firing would occur only when the propeller was clear of the path of the bullets. The combat pilot could then aim his weapon by aiming the airplane.

Squadrons by mid-1918 were organized into three sections (flights) of six airplanes each. Groups comprised three to five squadrons, normally four. The next level of organization was the wing that consisted of a variable number of groups. Tactically, observation and reconnaissance methods developed first, followed by pursuit (fighter) methods by late 1915, and long-distance bombardment and day bombardment by 1918. Night reconnaissance did not develop until the spring of 1918. Liaison with infantry units was the slowest to develop and was not perfected by the time of the Armistice. During the St. Mihiel and Meuse–Argonne campaigns, more than 1,000 aircraft of many types were deployed for reconnaissance, observation, and adjustment of artillery fire and bombardment. Aviation as an independent combat arm was close at hand.

Tank tactics

Tanks, like artillery, were infantry support units in the World War. In the French tank forces, artillery nomenclature was used to identify the heavy tank units—*groupement* instead of company and *group* instead of battalion. In both early battles at Cantigny (May 1918) and Soissons (July 1918), French tanks with French crews supported the American operations. At Cantigny the 5th Group (battalion) of 12 Schneider heavy tanks, organized into three "batteries" (*groupement* or company-sized units) of 4 tanks each, attacked from west to east on the left (north) of the American infantry line. Their advance was on either side of the village cemetery on the north side of Cantigny. In this early action the French tanks were an

appendage to the infantry formations, not integrated with them. "The American Infantry furnished 12 men to each Battery for Liaison. These men performed their duties perfectly—2 wounded." The commander of the French *groupement* was an officer named Forsanz. He reported that the artillery and the tanks were mutually supporting, but the tanks had extreme control difficulties when operating in low light levels. Moreover the approach march to the line of departure "could not be completely masked from observation" by the enemy. The early morning fog rising from a creek plus the dust raised by the shelling did give the tanks some concealment. Foranz observed that "the American Infantry showed a remarkable knowledge of how to use Tank assistance, following them closely without allowing themselves to be held up by them, and sticking close to their barrage." Experiments during the battle with a tank-towed fuel trailer and periscopes showed that more work was needed to make the techniques fully successful.

Three stalwart flying officers of the American Air Service. Left to right: 1st Lieutenant E. V. Rickenbacker, 1st Lieutenant Douglas Campbell (the first American ace) and Captain Kenneth Marr. Photo taken near Toul, France, on June 14, 1918. (US Signal Corps, 15819)

Later, in the St. Mihiel and Meuse–Argonne fighting, the American tank formations were more closely coordinated with the infantry assault. The technique worked out was to use heavy tanks in the van to crush the enemy wire, create lanes for the infantry, and destroy enemy machine-gun emplacements. The tanks moved closely behind a rolling barrage, but then waited for the infantry and light tanks to come forward before continuing the advance. At St. Mihiel (September 12–16, 1918) the Americans discovered the difference between training and combat. The results were disappointing. In order to be effective, the tanks must be able to maneuver. Heavy rains began to fall in the operational area the week prior to the jump-off date creating a 3ft-deep gelatinous slime in places. Small streams were over their banks. Additionally, the German trenches were wider than the 6ft span capability of the Renaults. The well-coordinated attack that Patton had planned soon broke down into small fights involving one or two tanks and very determined crewmembers. At this point, Patton's emphasis on training for his junior officers and noncommissioned officers paid off. The American soldier was at his best when improvising on the battlefield in the face of changing conditions. In addition to maneuverability, tanks relied on the firepower of their cannon and machine guns with the crew protected by the armor plate. The tanks still in action were running out of fuel and ammunition, necessitating some more battlefield innovation to bring the supplies forward. Communication between tanks and infantry soldiers was line of sight, all hampered by the smoke and noise of battle.

In the evening of September 14, the Tank Corps was alerted for redeployment to the Meuse–Argonne area to the north, part of Colonel George Marshall's masterful realignment of First Army from one battle area to another while still engaged. Losses to enemy action were light. Three tanks had been destroyed by enemy artillery fire, but 40 were stuck in the mud or broken down. The Germans had begun a general withdrawal from the St. Mihiel salient at the beginning of the American attack so a test of the tanks in the face of determined enemy resistance still lay ahead in the difficult terrain between the heights of the Meuse River and the Argonne Forest. At the end of the war Major General James McAndrew, AEF chief of staff, argued that the tank forces must "train with the infantry and become part of the infantry" in order to assist the infantry with that most difficult task of "actual closing with the enemy and the occupation of the enemy's position." Rockenbach, Patton, and their fellow tankers had made a good start.

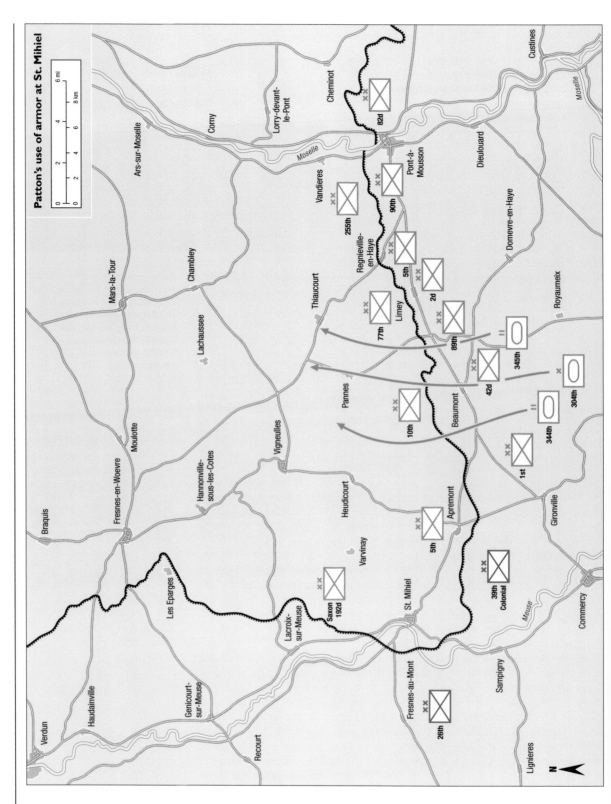

Nine American divisions led an attack against the St. Mihiel salient where the German Army had been entrenched since the beginning of the war. Two battalions of tanks were operating in support of the 89th and 42d Divisions. Lt. Col. George Patton commanded the 304th Tank Brigade, which had moderate success against an enemy that was already vacating the salient two days before the American attack.

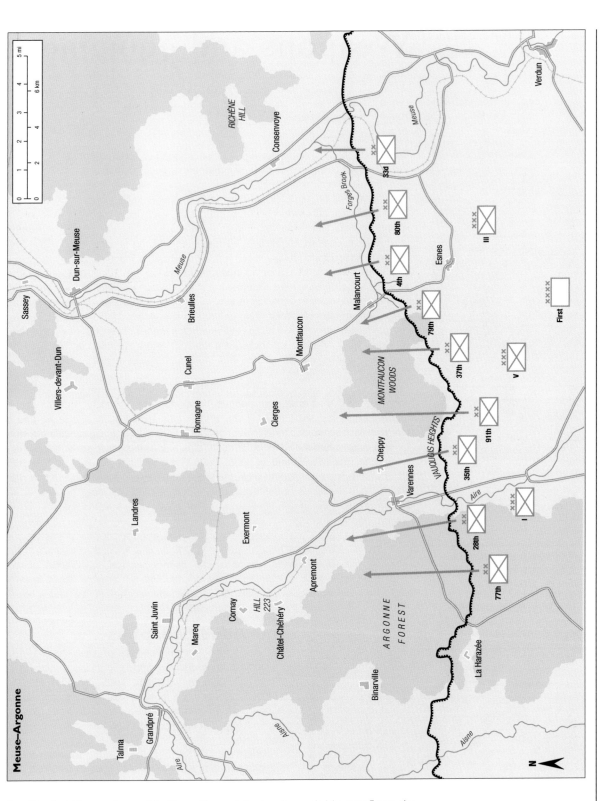

Meuse–Argonne

Attacking the high ground east of the Meuse River and the densely wooded Argonne Forest, the Americans launched their final offensive of the war on September 26 against the formidable obstacles of Montfaucon, Cunel, and Barricourt. The initial assault was slow and incurred many casualties. After a week, the Americans re-grouped and the high ground once held by the Germans was in Allied hands by November 5.

Weapons and equipment

Equipment

During the St. Mihiel operation in mid-September 1918, Herbert McHenry's machine-gun company carried only their battle packs containing a razor, comb, toothbrush, towel, soap, mess kit, and two days' rations. The combat rations were "four tins of hardtack containing four ounces each of hardtack, and two pounds of canned corned beef." Additionally, each man carried a bolo and a shovel or pick. The American soldier, in most instances, was suitably equipped for infantry combat in France, although the winter-service wool olive-drab uniform was stiff and heavy when wet, and unusable when doused with gas.

Two doughboys of the 28th Infantry Regiment undergoing trench warfare training near Gondrecourt, France, in July 1917. Note the heavy loads carried by each soldier. (US Signal Corps, 80114)

"Delousing" at the Army Sanitary Schools, Langres, France. Live steam was the best way to clean clothing and bedding, but it often left uniforms several sizes smaller as a result. Soldiers needed to be careful not to don the clean gear too soon after emerging from the cleaning trailer. (US Signal Corps, 49562)

The uniform consisted of a campaign or service hat (later replaced by the British tin helmet of 1916 design), a service coat or sweater, service breeches, olive-drab flannel shirt, canvas or leather leggings (replacing the puttee legging wraps, six million of which were ordered in the spring of 1918), russet leather shoes, identification tag, and, in cold weather, a pair of olive-drab woolen gloves.

The soldier's service kit included a field kit and a surplus kit. The field kit included personal clothing, arms and equipment consisting of a first-aid packet in a pouch, a canteen with cup and cover, a bacon can, a condiment can, a pack carrier, and a haversack, except if mounted. There also was a meat can, utensils, and half of a tent with one pole and five tent pins. Finally there was one identification tag with tape. If the soldier was armed with a rifle he had a bayonet with scabbard, a rifle sling, and a cartridge belt. If armed with a pistol, he would have had a holster for the side arm, a double-pocket magazine pouch, two extra magazines, and a pistol belt. The mounted enlisted soldier had additional horse equipment, more personal items, spurs, a scabbard for his rifle and 90 to 100 rounds of ball ammunition, reserve rations, one "housewife" (a mending kit) per squad, and some hand tools. The surplus kit had extra clothing and a folding rifle-cleaning rod in a case. These kits were packed in bags, one for each squad, one for sergeants, and one for cooks and buglers.

The 1917 *Manual for Noncommissioned Officers and Privates of Infantry of the Army of the United States* was a model primer written with great clarity in instructional style. It covered a host of topics in remarkable detail in only 350 small-format pages. Even an English–French vocabulary list and a blank last will and testament form were included.

Individual weapons

The basic arm for the soldiers of the AEF was the bolt-action, magazine-fed Springfield rifle model 1903. It weighed 9.69lb with the 16in. bayonet affixed. The soldier carried a basic "load" of 60 rounds of .30-cal. ball ammunition. The cartridges were packed five to a clip, 12 clips per cloth bandolier, weighing just under 4lb.

Nearly 600,000 Springfields, enough to equip a field army of one million men, were on hand in 1917. The problem was that nearly four million soldiers would be called to arms. The available rifles were used to outfit the early organizing Regular Army and National Guard divisions. About 200,000 Krag-Jörgensen Norwegian-made rifles, the standard rifle of the US Army from 1893 to 1903, were on hand. A British-designed Enfield

rifle, chambered for the US .30-cal. round, was put into production in August 1917 to take advantage of the existing manufacturing facilities that had been turning out Enfields for the British Army. Some units exchanged their issued rifles for another model upon arrival in France.

Some soldiers and all officers carried the US semi-automatic pistol, Colt .45-cal. model 1911. This sidearm had been developed in response to the experiences in the Philippines where "knock-down" power was needed to deal with the headlong charges of the Moros. The Colt .45 delivered the goods.

Automatic weapons

Heavy machine guns used by the AEF were of American design but usually of foreign manufacture. All the major inventors of machine guns—Hiram Maxim, Benjamin Hotchkiss, Isaac Lewis, and John Browning—were Americans, some of whom had taken their wares to Europe to seek a market prior to World War I. The early machine gun of American manufacture, the Benét-Mercié, did not compare favorably with the very good guns manufactured by Maxim, Hotchkiss, and Browning. At 30lb it was simply too heavy for infantry use. Lewis and Hotchkiss guns were successfully adapted for use in aircraft during the war.

As noted in the chapter on organization, machine-gun units were under-represented in the TO&E of the American division prior to June 1917, with only four guns authorized for the infantry regiment. Because of the reports of the Baker Board and other observers in Great Britain and France, the AEF quickly augmented its organization with more machine guns. By war's end the allocation of machine guns to the regiment had risen to 336. At the outset of US involvement in the war the machine gun was described as a weapon normally thought of as a defensive armament because of its weight, high consumption of ammunition, and the need for a large number of soldiers to service the gun. By the time of the Soissons operation in July 1918, however, the value of machine guns properly employed in the attack was clear.

Initially the American infantry units were equipped with the French Chauchat light machine gun, usually identified as an automatic rifle. The Chauchat was not the favorite weapon of the doughboy. Its 19lb weight and rapidly overheating barrels were its two main drawbacks. The Chauchat had a distinctive "banana-shaped" curved magazine that fed its 20 rounds of Lebel 8mm ammunition from the bottom of the gun. Joseph Dorst Patch said of the Chauchat that it simply was "no good." On the other hand, the Hotchkiss heavy machine gun "turned out to be the best machine gun of the war." Herbert McHenry was a Hotchkiss gun crewman in the 16th Infantry Regiment's machine-gun company. The company comprised three platoons, each with four squads of one machine gun per squad. Two-thirds of the company strength of 96 men had been put out of action in the Soissons operation and McHenry was a replacement. The company had 12 gun carts and

Troops from the 18th Infantry Regiment firing Hotchkiss 8mm machine guns in practice firing at Gondrecourt, August 20, 1917. (US Signal Corps, 80014)

Private R. E. Brenton, 4th Infantry Regiment, 3d Division, tries to discharge a captured German machine gun near Mount St. Père northeast of Château-Thierry during the Aisne–Marne campaign, July 22, 1918. (US Signal Corps, 17478)

12 ammunition carts, each drawn by one small mule. There were two caissons and two escort wagons, also drawn by mules, to haul the rest of the company's equipment and forage for the animals. McHenry remembered that there were 49 mules and five horses in the company. His squad had eight men at full strength. During the St. Mihiel operation McHenry was an ammunition carrier. He "toted" two boxes of Hotchkiss ammunition, each with 288 rounds weighing about 30lb. In his squad there were five ammunition carriers. The corporal carried the spare parts kit, the gunner carried the gun, and his loader carried the tripod, each weighing about 60lb.

Artillery

The three artillery regiments of the infantry division's artillery brigade consisted of two regiments of "light" Schneider 75mm guns (24 per regiment) and one regiment of "heavy" Schneider 155mm howitzers (24 pieces). A trench mortar battery of 12 tubes rounded out the artillery brigade commander's "organic" fire support. Heavier calibers of artillery were placed in the operational control of division artillery or supported by grouping units from corps and army artillery units with the American regiments.

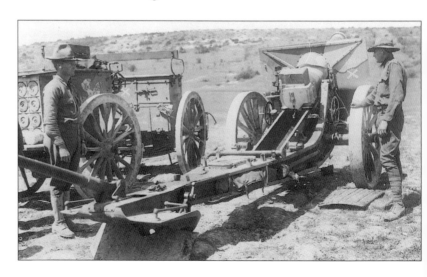

A Schneider 155mm howitzer of Battery C, 121st Artillery, at the II Corps School during artillery practice firing on the road near Latrecey southwest of Chaumont (photo taken May 24, 1918). The 121st Artillery Regiment was the heavy artillery of the 32d Division's artillery brigade. (US Signal Corps, 13975)

The French 75mm model 1897 was a revolutionary field gun. It was quick firing using fixed ammunition with a hydro-pneumatic recoil system and a trail spade to stabilize the gun during firing. It fired a 17.5lb shell to a maximum range of 10,600 yards at a rate of fire of 15 to 20 rounds per minute. The regiments armed with the 75mm normally fired the rolling barrages because of their high rate of fire.

The medium artillery regiment of the infantry division would have been equipped with the US-manufactured 4.7in. and 6in. guns but there were not enough of these guns to issue to deploying divisions. US factories produced only 2,766 75mm guns and 492 155mm guns, with the majority coming off production lines in 1919 after the Armistice. Accordingly the AEF equipped its artillery units arriving in France with French guns and French ammunition. Heavier artillery, to include naval guns mounted on railway cars, supported combat operations. 8in. howitzers of British design were manufactured at the Midvale Steel and Ordnance Company in Nicetown, Pennsylvania, and 123 British guns were received in France from the Vickers Company. The 8in. howitzer could throw a 200lb projectile nearly seven miles. Larger-caliber howitzers were planned, but the war ended before they could be brought to the field. In World War I most belligerents were able to field a small number of naval-style guns, but their utility depended upon the ability of the armies to build rail spurs in order to move the guns within range of their targets. The US Ordnance Department made nearly 300 railway guns, but few were ready by the time of the Armistice. Unlike the German "Big Bertha" that shelled Paris from 70 miles away, the US Navy's 14in. railroad guns could be fired from their cars within ten minutes of arriving in position. The American guns could fire a 1,400lb shell at a range of 45,000 yards. One locomotive and 13 cars were needed to put one gun into action. Five of these units were located at corps and army levels and were ready for action by mid-September 1918 in the Meuse–Argonne campaign.

Armored fighting vehicles

As has been mentioned previously, tanks of American manufacture did not make it to France in time to participate in combat operations. Manufacturing schedules were pointed toward delivering light and medium tanks of French and British design for the 1919 campaign year. Approximately 1,100 5- and 10-ton tractors, used to tow medium and heavy artillery pieces, had been shipped to France by November 1, 1918, and a smaller number of larger tractors had been secured from British and French sources.

Rail and truck transport

Railroads in the United States were critical to the war effort. Movement of materiel and troops from factories and encampments to the ports required central control. President Wilson appointed his son-in-law, William McAdoo, to be director general of the US Railroad Administration to provide organization and direction to the effort. Overseas, locomotives, and rolling stock of standard gauge were needed in and around the port areas, but the French intercity rail system was sufficient to move men and supplies from the ports to the front. The army engineers managed the construction of rail lines and the operation of the port rail facilities. Special engineer regiments built narrow-gauge rail systems to connect the French railheads with the rear service areas of the theaters of operation. In addition to moving troops and equipment, ammunition and food, the light rail systems were used to evacuate wounded soldiers. Nearly 125 miles of light rail lines employed 406 locomotives and 2,385 cars.

The Assistant Chief-of-Staff, G-4, AEF, and the Commanding General, Services of Supply, were the staff planner and operator respectively for the AEF's transport needs. At GHQ, AEF, Brigadier General George Van Horn Moseley served as the G-4. A Director General of Transportation and a Director of Motor Transportation served as special staff officers to oversee the important function that kept the supply and maintenance of the army flowing effectively. The motor vehicle may have been the most important piece of equipment contributing to the Allied victory in France. As with aircraft, the army learned important lessons about trucks from their experiences in 1916 during the Mexican punitive expedition. The Quartermaster Corps understood that standardization was important, but the demands of the war could not wait for that development. Several hundred makes of motor vehicles were pressed into service. Reliability and maintainability were critical. Trucks, ambulances, motorcycles, and bicycles of all sorts were procured from the French and British, in addition to the approximately 33,000 trucks from $3/4$-ton to 5-ton capacity that arrived from the US. Nearly 10,000 Standard B trucks of 3–5-ton capacity were produced in the US before the Armistice. Most of the major American companies—Ford, Dodge, Cadillac, General Motors, and White—produced trucks. "In 1917 and 1918 nearly 100,000 trucks and chassis, about 15,000 ambulances and 18,000 passenger cars, 65,000 motorcycles with side cars, and 68,000 bicycles were delivered to the Army." Each infantry division had about 650 trucks integral to its organization. Rails, wheels, and hooves propelled the AEF into battle.

Aircraft

Aviation began as a very small enterprise in the US military system. In the army, a handful of airplanes purchased from the Wright brothers were managed by the Signal Corps. On the eve of the departure of the AEF for Europe, the French were flying 1,700 combat aircraft at the battle front. Just as with artillery, the American aviation units, as they were formed, started operations with French and British aircraft. A full year prior to the entry of the United States as an "associated power" with the Allied coalition, American volunteer pilots were flying French Nieuports and Spads. But US industrial capabilities did not match the dreams and plans of the War Department. By July 1917 fewer than 100 planes had rolled off the factory lines. Bureaucratic inefficiencies and lack of central control over design and resources prevented rapid progress in building the American air fleet. In June 1917 Major Raynal C. Bolling led a large team of technical evaluators to Europe to pick out the best models so that they could be manufactured in the United States. He chose the British Bristol and the French Spad, both fighters, the British De Havilland DH-4 for observation and day bombardment, and the Italian Caproni for night bombardment. Only the DH-4 survived the tangle of competing agencies and interests. By May 1918 better control over aviation matters came with the creation of the Bureau of Aircraft Production with copper entrepreneur John D. Ryan at its head. This agency, along with a Bureau of Military Aeronautics headed by Major General William L. Kenly, promised to give the War Department the administrative capability it had lacked. But in practice, coordination just never happened before the Armistice ended hostilities.

Prior to April 1917 the United States built perhaps 800 airplanes for foreign contracts, all for training not combat. By the end of hostilities, 8,567 training aircraft (of a total of 11,754) had been produced in American factories. For pilot basic instruction the Curtiss JN-4 and the Standard Aero Corporation J-1 were used. The JN-4 was the superior aircraft for training purposes. Because of the concentration on the training machines where the nation's factories had production experience and because the US lacked

General Tasker H. Bliss and Major General James G. Harbord with John D. Ryan, Director of Aircraft Production, on the steps of General Harbord's quarters in Tours. (US Signal Corps, 23817)

expertise in the design and construction of combat, or service, planes, the fighting aircraft had to be procured abroad while the manufacturing base caught up.

By the time the first American-built DH-4s reached the front in August 1918, they were already obsolete. The location of the fuel tank in the center of the fuselage between the pilot and the observer led to some in-flight fires and the unattractive nickname of "flying or flaming coffin." Just over 400 of the DH-4s were flown as observation and day bombardment squadrons of the Air Service.

The American Liberty engine had better success. Although raw materials prevented the efficient production of airframes, engines were a different engineering challenge, with weight per horsepower being the hardest to solve. Most European-design aircraft engines, notably the Rolls-Royce products, were evolving quickly with many design changes. The US had to get out in front of the normal production lead time of over a year with a stable, innovative design. What became known as the "Liberty" engine was designed in late May 1917 in guest rooms at the Willard Hotel in Washington, DC, in a matter of days. By early June the Aircraft Production Board approved the design and on July 4 the first 8-cylinder engine arrived in the nation's capital, but it was soon evident that the 12-cylinder engine approaching 400 horsepower was to be the standard. The Packard Motor Car Company and Ford Motor Company produced most of the engines. Extraordinary cooperation among rival manufacturing companies and the decision of the US government to pool all the relevant design features and underwrite royalties were major features of the production process. At the time of the Armistice, 150 engines a day were pouring off the production lines. The engines weren't cheap—about $7,000 each, 15 times the cost of an automobile.

A top view of the American-built De Havilland D-H4 "flying coffin" airplane. This image offers a good view of the Liberty engine. (US Signal Corps, 8476)

Armistice, occupation, recovery, and demobilization

Officers of the 1st Division observe the 26th Infantry Regiment crossing the Armistice line at Etain, November 17, 1918. Left to right: Brigadier General Frank Parker, Brigadier General Francis C. Marshall, Lieutenant Colonel Theodore Roosevelt, Jr., Captain M. H. Lane, and Major T. R. Gowenlock. (US Signal Corps, 35055)

Monday, November 11, 1918, was a day that all American doughboys remembered. They could recall exactly what they were doing and where they were when they learned about the end of the war. Max Ottenfeld, a "professional" private in the 18th Infantry, had been released from the hospital where he was being treated for gas injuries earlier that day. As he marched forward to find his unit, headquarters, and headquarters company, he began to see French soldiers in a high state of excitement. All were shouting about the end of the war. Max finally got a ride forward and eventually found his unit, which would soon be in the Coblenz occupation sector of Germany.

But the Armistice, a temporary suspension of hostilities, was not victory. The Central Powers had not been defeated by the annihilation, capture, or surrender of their field armies. Peacemaking proceeded from the formal surrender at Compiègne as the belligerent powers gathered at Versailles. The Americans, while represented at the Supreme War Council by Colonel Edward House and General Tasker H. Bliss, were not at the table in Marshal Foch's railroad car in the grove of trees northeast of Paris. General Pershing and selected members of his staff had met with Marshal Foch at his headquarters at Senlis on October 28. Pershing expressed the view that surrender of the German armies, not an armistice, should be the goal. Pétain, on the other hand, believed that the best way to render the German field armies impotent was to deprive them of their materiel. Rolling stock, guns, and

Officers of the 1st Division at Boppard, Germany, on the Rhine River, December 10, 1918. Major General Edward F. McGlachlin, Jr., commander 1st Division at left with cigar. Lieutenant Colonel Ted Roosevelt, Jr. at right with cane. (US Signal Corps, 39638)

ammunition were to be left behind as the armies withdrew beyond the Rhine. General Harbord at his SOS headquarters received word of the cessation of hostilities at about 0900hrs and sent the band of the 13th Marine Regiment to the quarters of the French prefect and the French regional commander to play "the patriotic airs of the Allied Nations, and the best and gayest music that it knew." As president of an associated power in the war effort, President Wilson desired to remain aloof from the entanglements of political negotiations underway at the end of the fighting. At Versailles, however, he was the only head of state to take an active part in the formulation of the treaties that ended the war.

The Third US Army under the command of Major General Dickman, later to be re-designated the American Forces in Germany, marched into the Grand Duchy of Luxemburg on November 17 and across the Rhine River into the Rhineland on December 1, 1918. The process of occupation, demobilization, and disposal of stored materiel had begun.

Von Hindenburg, the first American horse to drink from the Rhine River near Boppard, Germany, December 10, 1918. The rider is Captain M.W. Lanham, 2d Infantry Brigade, 1st Division. (US Signal Corps, 39639)

Occupation of Germany by American forces lasted until July 2, 1919, when Third Army was discontinued, with remaining small forces transferred to AFG or SOS. The AFG took over occupation duties on July 3, 1919, with Major General McGlachlin, Jr., former commander of the 1st Division at the end of hostilities, then Major General Henry T. Allen, former commander of the 90th Division, in command. The AFG terminated occupation duties on January 11, 1923, and left Coblenz on January 24. General Allen turned operations over to General Marty of the French Army on January 27. The great leap overseas that had begun in June 1917 had drawn to a close.

General Pershing, despite pressure from the other Allied nations, notably France, had fixed the size of the occupying forces at 15 divisions on April 1, 1919, with reduction to ten by May 1. The French ports of Brest, St. Nazaire, and Bordeaux that had been used to receive the AEF acted in reverse fashion to embark the Americans for the trip home. A major out-processing center was established at Le Mans because the facilities at Brest and St. Nazaire were inadequate. The troops referred to this process as going through "the mill." Harbord put a competent officer in charge at Brest, Marine Colonel Smedley D. Butler, known as "General Duckboard" to the departing troops because he liberated 80,000 sections of duckboard from American quartermasters who

1st Division on parade in Washington, DC, September 17, 1919. Wounded veterans moving to their seats in the grandstand. The Big Red One had paraded down Fifth Avenue in New York City on September 10. (US Signal Corps, 63698)

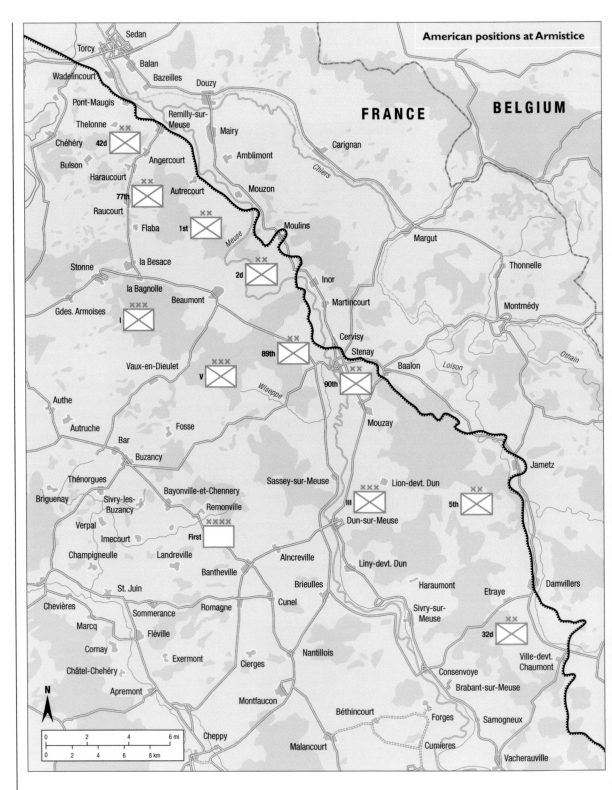

FRANCE

BELGIUM

Sedan
Torcy
Balan
Wadelincourt
Bazeilles
Douzy
Pont-Maugis
Remilly-sur-
Meuse
Thelonne
Mairy
Chéhéry   42d
Carignan
Angercourt
Amblimont
Bulson
Haraucourt   77th
Autrecourt
Mouzon
Raucourt
Flaba   1st
Moulins
Margut
la Besace
Meuse
Stonne
la Bagnolle   2d
Inor
Thonnelle
Gdes. Armoises   I
Beaumont
Martincourt
Montmédy
Vaux-en-Dieulet   V   89th
Cervisy
Stenay
Baalon
Loison
Othain
Authe
Wiseppe   90th
Autruche
Fosse
Mouzay
Bar
Buzancy
Jametz
Thénorgues
Sassey-sur-Meuse
Lion-devt. Dun
Briguenay
Bayonville-et-Chennery
III   5th
Sivry-les-
Buzancy
Remonville
Dun-sur-Meuse
Verpal
First
Imecourt
Alncreville
Champigneulle
Landreville
Liny-devt. Dun
Bantheville
Brieulles
St. Juin
Cunel
Haraumont
Etraye
Damvillers
Chevières
Romagne
Marcq
Sommerance
Sivry-sur-
Meuse
Fléville
Cornay
Exermont
Cierges
Nantillois
32d
Châtel-Chéhéry
Ville-devt.
Chaumont
Apremont
Consenvoye
Montfaucon
Brabant-sur-Meuse
N
Béthincourt
Forges
Samogneux
0   2   4   6 mi
Cheppy
0   2   4   6   8 km
Malancourt
Cumières
Vacherauville

By November 11 the American forces had penetrated the Antwerp–Meuse line, the German third and last line of defense. Most of the American divisions had crossed the Meuse River, and two, the 1st and 42d, had reached Sedan and were in the process of taking the city before being ordered to withdraw in order to give the French the right of way. When halted by the Armistice the 5th Division was within artillery range of the German Lines of Communication.

were saving them for use at the bottom of trenches, organized the facilities at Brest, got the troops up out of the mud, and used the resources of his regiment to care for troops afflicted with influenza. The last division to leave the Coblenz sector for the United States was the 1st Division—the same division that was the first into action on May 28, 1918, at Cantigny. On August 8, 1919, the 1st, minus some of its small units that remained with the AFG, was transferred to General Harbord's SOS. It embarked on the SS *Orizaba* at Brest on August 22 and arrived at the port of Hoboken, New Jersey, on August 30. In September, to show the American people their fighting division, the 1st paraded in both Washington and New York City. The operations order for the New York City parade was considerably longer than that which put the division into action at Cantigny! Peace had broken out.

Smiling doughboy with his mess kit and canteen cup at Gondrecourt. The original Signal Corps caption said "One of 'Uncle Sam's' well fed soldiers." (US Signal Corps, 80108)

Toast to the Allies at PC Moscou, France, April 16, 1918. The American doughboy and the French poilu symbolized the Allied coalition. (US Signal Corps, 12145)

Private Max Ottenfeld, signal wireman, 18th Infantry Regiment, 1st Division. (MRC)

Retrospective

Lessons subsume recognition, analysis, and implementation. Lessons from the American participation in World War I had both positive and negative influences on the interwar army in the United States. The most effective lessons were administrative and logistical; the least effective were organizational, doctrinal, and tactical.

America's great citizen-soldier army had made its mark in France, but the mark was one of Yankee determination, grim resolution, and individual combativeness. Organizations within the AEF had developed, changed, matured, and in some cases proved less than effective. The record of combat and administrative leadership was a good one overall. The Meuse–Argonne campaign had challenged the American army and its AEF to its elastic limits. It was without question the largest and most complex military operation in the history of the American army since its Civil War. General Pershing and his staff skilfully dealt with new dimensions such as toxic gas warfare, aerial and tank combat, and coalition warfare.

Following the termination of hostilities in 1918 until his death in 1948, John J. Pershing presided over a small group of protégés—John L. Hines, Charles P. Summerall, Malin Craig, and George C. Marshall, all destined to be chiefs-of-staff of the US Army. A larger group of contemporaries and junior officers shaped the army of the interwar years so that when the emergency that became World War II arrived the army was able to mobilize, organize, deploy, and fight. Throughout that period John Pershing remained an advisor to presidents and War Department officials. It can be said without fear of much exaggeration that the 30 years following World War I in the United States were the years of John J. Pershing as much as those of any single American.

The losses of life and property in the World War were staggering. The United States suffered 50,300 men killed in battle compared with 1,700,000 Russians, 1,600,000 Germans, and 1,385,000 French. Of the major belligerent nations, only Greece and Portugal lost fewer soldiers than the Americans. The infantry bore more than half of all the battle deaths, followed by the signal corps, engineers, artillery, and tank crewmen. Among officers, the infantry counted 80 percent of the losses, followed by flying officers. Wounded soldiers always outnumber those killed outright in battle. Death from wounds comprised almost 30 percent of the total battle deaths, but the wounded were four times the dead. The total American battle casualties in all categories were 260,496.

Comparable with battle losses, however, were the losses to disease, including the great influenza pandemic that swept the ranks of all armies in 1918. Pneumonia caused 40,000 deaths, 25,000 associated with the flu pandemic in both the camps stateside and in the AEF. From mid-September 1918 to the armistice nearly 370,000 cases of influenza and pneumonia struck down troops in the United States. Disease caused 50 percent of the total dead from all causes in the American Army and Navy, but this was the first war "that showed a lower death rate from disease than from battle." The entire army was vaccinated against typhoid fever plus medical and sanitary services were vastly improved from previous wars.

The economic consequences of the war were substantial for the United States. The cost of maintaining an armed forces of more than four million was more than one million dollars per hour for 25 months—about 21.85 billion dollars attributable to the war. The army accounted for about two-thirds of that total. Forty-four cents of every dollar spent by the army went for quartermaster

Two views of the reunion of the 1st Division at Camp Dix, New Jersey, November 11, 1920. The Cantigny "fort" and the Soissons "arch." (MRC)

items, 29 cents for guns and ammunition, 6 cents for the Air Service and 13 cents for soldiers' pay. Another 8.85 billion dollars were advanced as loans to the various Allied nations. Of course the war and the US army could not stop on the dime once hostilities ceased. There were huge stocks of supplies, munitions, and equipment in both France and the United States that had to be dealt with. There were outstanding contracts that had to be cancelled or diverted to other ends. Airplanes, Liberty engines, tanks, trucks, artillery pieces, rifles, machine guns, and a host of other materiel were on hand. This had the downside effect of creating an aura of military security and a disincentive to continue to develop and produce military hardware. Nearly 1,000 6-ton tanks of the Renault light tank design had been manufactured, but not one made it into action in France prior to the Armistice. The National Defense Act of 1920 allocated those tanks to the infantry branch of the army, leaving the tank corps without mission or equipment. George Patton was so discouraged that he returned to the cavalry branch in the interwar period.

Without question, the real heroes of the AEF in France were the American service personnel. While institutions, policies, and strategies were in flux, the infantry soldier and marine did what was expected of him, despite accelerated and often inadequate training, despite often mediocre leadership at the lowest levels, and despite shortages of equipment.

The United States joined the war in progress at the moment of the Allies' greatest need. Americans, British, and French soldiers carried the burden of combat from May 28, 1918, forward to the Armistice on November 11, 1918, together. Brigadier General Fox Conner, the operations officer of the AEF, concluded his report of July 2, 1919, by reminding us that the one great lesson of the war was "the unprepared nation is helpless in a great war unless it can depend upon other nations to shield it while it prepares." He was not confident that the nation would long remember it. The lesson of successful coalition warfare is perhaps the most significant outcome of the war for the United States.

The New York City parade of the 1st Division, September 10, 1919. (MRC)

Chronology

1903

14 February	Army General Staff Corps created by act of Congress

1916

7 March	Newton D. Baker replaces Lindley M. Garrison as Secretary of War
9 March	Pancho Villa raids Columbus, New Mexico, killing 17
15 March	Brigadier General John J. Pershing heads a "punitive expedition" to catch Villa
3 June	National Defense Act expands Regular Army, authorizes National Guard, creates ROTC, and strengthens industrial preparedness
7 November	Woodrow Wilson elected to a second term the on slogan "he kept us out of war"

1917

6 April	US declares war on Germany
18 May	Selective Service Act
26 May	Major General Pershing appointed commander-in-chief, AEF
13 June	Major General Pershing arrives in Paris and sets up AEF Headquarters
26–30 June	1st Division arrives at St. Nazaire
4 July	2d Battalion, 16th Infantry Regiment, parades down Champs Elysées in Paris
5 July	General Staff, AEF, created by General Orders No. 8
11 July	General Pershing approves the General Organization Project for the AEF
1 September	General Headquarters (GHQ), AEF, moves to Chaumont
3 November	F Company, 2d Battalion, 16th Infantry Regiment, loses first three soldiers in trench raid

1918

4 March	Peyton C. March becomes acting chief-of-staff, US Army
March–April	German spring offensives on the Western Front
28–31 May	Battle of Cantigny, first American offensive action of the war
17 July	President Wilson authorizes US forces to join Allied North Russian Expedition
18–22 July	Soissons operation of the Aisne–Marne counter-offensive
31 July	General Orders No. 1, First Army, designates Pershing as commander
6 August	Aisne–Marne salient cleared of Germans
10 August	Field Order No. 1, First Army, takes control of sector along Vesle River
15 August	27th Infantry Regiment arrives Vladivostok, Siberia, and organizes AEF Siberia HQ. 31st Infantry Regiment arrives within a week
12–16 September	St. Mihiel operation of First Army
26 September	Meuse–Argonne operation of First Army
5 November	Republicans gain control of both Houses of Congress
11 November	Armistice
1 December	Third Army enters Germany for occupation duty

1919

3 July	American Forces in Germany (AFG) replaces Third Army on occupation duty
22 August	American Forces in France (AFF) created to replace GHQ, AEF
22 August	1st Division embarks on the SS *Orizaba* at Brest for return home
10 September	1st Division parades in New York City
17 September	1st Division parades in Washington, DC

1923

24 January	AFG departs Coblenz, Germany, for home
27 January	Major General Henry T. Allen turns command of American zone of occupation over to French

Bibliography

The bibliography that follows is not comprehensive, only representative of the variety of works in English that are readily available, either by purchase or loan from good libraries. The best general source on the history of the US Army is that of the late Russell F. Weigley. The best specialized source on the American Expeditionary Forces is Edward M. Coffman's *The War To End All Wars*. For the logistical story, James Harbord's memoir, *The American Army In France, 1917–1919*, clearly is the best. The best first-person source is that of George C. Marshall, *Memoirs of My Services in the World War 1917–1918*. The remaining titles fill in the story with detail and explanation.

American Armies and Battlefields in Europe. Washington, DC: Center of Military History, United States Army, 1992 [1927, 1938 by American Battle Monuments Commission].

Ayers, Leonard P. *The War with Germany: A Statistical Summary*, 2nd edition. Washington, DC: Government Printing Office, 1919.

Barbeau, Arthur E., and Henri, Florette. *The Unknown Soldiers: African-American Troops in World War I*. New York: Da Capo Press, 1996.

Braim, Paul F. *The Test Of Battle: The American Expeditionary Forces in the Meuse–Argonne Campaign*. Newark: University of Delaware Press, 1987.

Bruce, Robert B. *A Fraternity of Arms: America & France in the Great War*. Lawrence, KS: The University Press of Kansas, 2003.

Buck, Beaumont B. *Memories of Peace and War*. San Antonio, TX: The Naylor Company, 1925.

Bullard, Robert Lee. *Personalities and Reminiscences of the War*. Garden City, NY: Doubleday, Page, 1925.

Coffman, Edward M. *The War To End All Wars: The American Military Experience in World War I*. New York: Oxford University Press, 1968.

Crowell, Benedict and Wilson, Robert Forrest. *How America Went to War*. 6 volumes. New Haven, CT: Yale University Press, 1921.

Dickman, Joseph Theodore. *The Great Crusade: A Narrative of the World War*. New York: D. Appleton and Company, 1927.

Eisenhower, John S. D. *Yanks: The Epic Story of the American Army in World War I*. New York: The Free Press, 2001.

Evans, Martin M. *Retreat Hell! We Just Got Here!: The American Expeditionary Force in France, 1917–1918*. Oxford: Osprey Publishing, 1998.

Fleming, Thomas. *The Illusion of Victory: America in World War I*. New York: Basic Books, 2003.

Greenwood, Paul. *The Second Battle of the Marne 1918*. Shrewsbury, England: Airlife Publishing Ltd., 1998.

Hallas, James H. *Doughboy War: The American Expeditionary Force in World War I*. Boulder, CO & London: Lynne Rienner Publishers, 2000.

_____. *Squandered Victory: The American First Army at St. Mihiel*. Westport, CT: Praeger, 1995.

Harbord, Major General James G. *Leaves from a War Diary*. New York: Dodd, Mead & Company, 1925.

_____. *The American Army in France 1917–1919*. Boston: Little, Brown, And Company, 1936.

Harries, Meirion and Susie. *The Last Days of Innocence: America at War 1917–1918*. New York: Random House, 1997.

Johnson, Douglas V. II and Hillman, Rolfe L., Jr. *Soissons 1918*. College Station, TX: Texas A&M University Press, 1999.

Keene, Jennifer D. *Doughboys, the Great War, and the Remaking of America*. Baltimore & London: The Johns Hopkins University Press, 2001.

Kennett, Lee. *The First Air War, 1914–1918*. New York: The Free Press, 1981.

Liggett, Hunter. *A.E.F.* New York: Dodd, Mead & Company, 1928.

_____. *Commanding an American Army: Recollections of the World War*. Boston: Houghton Mifflin Company, 1925.

March, General Peyton C. *The Nation At War*. Garden City, New York: Doubleday, Doran & Company, Inc., 1932.

Marshall, George C. *Memoirs of My Services in the World War 1917–1918*. Boston: Houghton Mifflin Company, 1976.

Mead, Gary. *The Doughboys: America and the First World War*. Woodstock & New York: The Overlook Press, 2000.

Millett, Allan R. *The General: Robert L. Bullard and Officership in the United States Army, 1881–1925*. Westport, CT: Greenwood Press, 1975.

Millett, Allan R. and Murray, Williamson, eds. *Military Effectiveness: Volume I: The First World War*. Boston: Unwin Hyman, 1989 (paper edition).

Mosier, John. *The Myth of the Great War: A New Military History of World War I*. New York: HarperCollins Publishers, 2001.

Nenninger, Timothy K. *The Leavenworth Schools and the Old Army: Education, Professionalism, and the Officer Corps of the United States Army, 1881–1918*. Westport, CT: Greenwood Press, 1978.

Sheffield, Gary. *Forgotten Victory: The First World War: Myths and Realities*. London: Headline Book Publishing, 2001.

The United States Army in World War I. A collection of primary documents in CD-ROM format. Washington, DC: Center Of Military History, United States Army, 1998.

Thomas, Shipley. *The History of the A.E.F.* Nashville: The Battery Press, 2000 [1920].

Trask, David F. *The AEF and Coalition Warmaking, 1917–1918*. Lawrence, KS: University Press of Kansas, 1993.

_____. *The United States in the Supreme War Council: American War Aims and Inter-Allied Strategy, 1917–1918*. Middletown, CT: Wesleyan University Press, 1961.

Weigley, Russell F., *History of the United States Army*, enlarged edition. Bloomington: University of Indiana Press, 1984.

Wilson, Dale E. *Treat 'Em Rough! The Birth of American Armor, 1917–20*. Novato, CA: Presidio Press, 1989.

Zieger, Robert H. *America's Great War: World War I and the American Experience*. Lanham, MD: Rowman & Littlefield Publishers, Inc., 2000.

Source Notes

The text for this book, *The AEF in World War I*, was prepared with footnotes to document the sources of quotations and ideas from others. Space has not permitted the inclusion of the full set of footnotes, although they are on file with the publisher. In this short section the author lists the sources of quoted material and selected interpretations of other scholars, as well of some of the archival sources relied upon. By means of this section and the bibliography, every effort has been made, consistent with the publisher's policies, to reveal the references to the published work of others. Any oversights are unintentional and entirely the responsibility of the author.

Introduction. Professor I. B. Holley, "The Chaumont Coterie," in *Cantigny at Seventy-Five* (Wheaton, IL: The Cantigny First Division Foundation, 1973); Timothy K. Nenninger, "'Unsystematic as a Mode of Command': Commanders and the Process of Command in the American Expeditionary Forces, 1917–1918," *The Journal of Military History*, 64 (July 2000) [hereafter *TKN*]; John J. Pershing, *My Experiences in the World War*, 2 vols. (New York: Frederick A. Stokes Company, 1931) [hereafter *JJPM*] and Pershing's *Final Report to the Secretary of War*, September 1, 1918 [hereafter *JJPFR*].

Mission. Russell F. Weigley, *History of the United States Army*, enlarged ed. (Bloomington, IN: Indiana University Press 1984) [hereafter *RFWArmy*]; *JJPM*.

Preparation for war. *United States Army in the World War 1917–1919*, 17 vols. (Washington, DC: Historical Division, Department of the Army, 1948) [hereafter *USAWW*]; National Archives and Records Administration, ARCH II, College Park, MD (Record Groups 120, 165 & 200); *JJPFR*; John Patrick Finnegan, *Against the Specter of a Dragon: The Campaign for American Military Preparedness, 1914–1917* (Westport, CT & London: Greenwood Press, 1974); Dale Van Every, *The A.E.F. in Battle* (New York & London: D. Appleton and Company, 1928); Anne Cipriano Venzon, ed., *The United States in the First World War: An Encyclopedia* (New York & London: Garland Publishing, Inc., 1995) [hereafter *ACV Ency.*]; Marvin A. Kreidberg and Merton G. Henry, *History of Military Mobilization in the United States Army 1775–1945* [DA Pamphlet 20-212] (Washington, DC: Department of the Army, Nov. 1955) [hereafter *K&H*]; *RFWArmy*; Frederick Palmer, *Newton D. Baker: America at War*, 2 vols. (New York: Dodd, Mead & Company, 1931) [hereafter *NDB*]; Colonel Oliver Lyman Spaulding and Colonel John Womack Wright, *The Second Division American Expeditionary Force* [sic.] *in France 1917–1919* (New York: The Hillman Press, Inc. for the Historical Committee, Second Division Association, 1937) [hereafter *2dDiv*]; Herbert L. McHenry, *As a Private Saw It: My Memories of the First Division World War I* (Indiana, PA: The A.G. Halldin Publishing Company, 1988) [hereafter *McHenry*]; Major General Joseph Dorst Patch, U.S. Army Ret'd, *A Soldier's War: The First Infantry Division, A.E.F. (1917-1918)* (Corpus Christi, TX: Mission Press, 1966) [hereafter *Patch*]; Benedict Crowell and Robert Forrest Wilson, *How America Went to War*, 6 vols. (New Haven, CT: Yale University Press, 1921) [hereafter *Crowell & Wilson*]; Historical Section, Army War College, *Order of Battle of the United States Land Forces in the World War: American Expeditionary Forces*, multi-vol. (Washington, DC: US Government Printing Office, 1937) [hereafter *OBUS*]; Allan R. Millett, *The General: Robert L. Bullard and Officership in the United States Army 1881–1925* (Westport, CT: Greenwood Press, 1975) [hereafter *Bullard*]; George C. Marshall, *Memoirs of My Services in the World War 1917-1918* (Boston: Houghton Mifflin Company, 1976) [hereafter *GCM*]; *History of the First Division during the World War 1917–1919* (Philadelphia: The Society of the First Division, 1922) [hereafter *1stDiv.*].

Command, control, communication, and intelligence. *RFWArmy*; *NDB*; James J. Cooke, *Pershing and his Generals: Command and Staff in the AEF* (Westport, CT: Praeger, 1997); *TKN*; *GCM*; Major General Hunter Liggett, *A.E.F.: Ten Years Ago In France* (New York: Dodd, Mead And Company, 1928) [hereafter *Liggett A.E.F.*]; *Harbord*; memoirs of Charles P. Summerall, Conrad Babcock and Beaumont Buck (Buck's was published, the other two are MSS).

Organization. *JJPM*; *NDB*; Frank E. Vandiver, *Black Jack: The Life and Times of John J. Pershing*, 2 vols. (College Station, TX & London: Texas A&M University Press, 1977) [hereafter *Black Jack*]; *K&H*; Irving B. Holley, Jr., *General John M. Palmer, Citizen Soldiers, and the Army of a Democracy* (Westport, CT & London: Greenwood Press, 1982); *OBUS*; James G. Harbord, *The American Army in France 1917–1919* (Boston: Little, Brown, and Company, 1936) [hereafter *Harbord*]; *USAWW*; *ACVEncy*; *RFWArmy*; Liggett A.E.F.; *The Genesis of The American First Army* (Washington, DC: Historical Section, Army War College, 1938) [hereafter *First Army*]; *JJPFR*; Edward M. Coffman, *The War To End All Wars: The American Military Experience in World War I* (Madison, WI: The University of Wisconsin Press, 1968) [hereafter *Coffman*]; Robert Lee Bullard, *Personalities and Reminiscences of the War* (Garden City, NY: Doubleday, Page & Company, 1925) [hereafter *RLB*]; Bert Ford, *The Fighting Yankees Overseas* (Boston: Norman E. McPhail, Publisher, 1919); Major J. O. Adler, ed., *History of the Seventy Seventh Division, August 25th, 1917, November 11th, 1918* (New York: The 77th Division Association, 1919) [hereafter *77th Div.*]; Dale E. Wilson, *Treat 'Em Rough! The Birth of American Armor, 1917–20* (Novato, CA: Presidio, 1989); Leonard P. Ayers, *The War with Germany: A Statistical Summary*, 2nd ed. (Washington, DC: Government Printing Office, 1919) [hereafter *Ayers*]; *OBUS*; Maj.Gen. M. W. Ireland, The Surgeon General, et.al., *The Medical Department of the United States Army in the World War*, 15 vols. (Washington: Government Printing Office, 1925).

Tactics. Donald Smythe, *Pershing: General of the Armies* (Bloomington, IN: Indiana University Press, 1986) [hereafter *Smythe*]; *RLB*; Hunter Liggett, *Commanding an American Army: Recollections of the World War* (Boston & New York: Houghton Mifflin Company, 1925) [hereafter *Liggett Commanding*]; *USAWW*; *TKN*; Allan R. Millett, "Cantigny, 28-31 May 1918," in Charles E. Heller and William A. Stofft, eds., *America's First Battles, 1776–1965* (Lawrence: University Press of Kansas, 1986) [hereafter *Cantigny*]; *JJPFR*; *GCM*; *World War Records First Division A.E.F. Regular*, multi-volume [hereafter *WWR*]; *Patch*; *McHenry*; Douglas V. Johnson II and Rolfe L. Hillman, Jr., *Soissons 1918* (College Station, TX: Texas A&M University Press, 1999) [hereafter *Soissons*]; James J. Hudson, *Hostile Skies: A Combat History of the American Air Service in World War I* (Syracuse, NY: Syracuse University Press, 1968) [hereafter *Hostile Skies*]; Maurer Maurer, ed., *The U.S. Air Service in World War I*, 4 vols. (Washington, DC: The Office of Air Force History, Headquarters USAF, 1978) [hereafter *Maurer Maurer*]; Lee Kennett, *The First Air War 1914–1918* (New York: The Free Press, 1991) [hereafter *Kennett*].

Weapons and equipment. *USAWW*; U.S. War Department, *Manual for Noncommissioned Officers and Privates of Infantry of the Army of the United States, 1917* (Washington, DC: Government Printing Office, 1917) [hereafter *Infantry Manual*]; *Ayers*; Crowell & Wilson; Patch; McHenry; Ian V. Hogg, *Allied Artillery of World War One* (Wiltshire, UK: The Crowood Press Ltd., 1998) [hereafter *Hogg Artillery*]; William G. Dooly, Jr., *Great Weapons of World War I* (New York: Bonanza Books, 1969) [hereafter *Dooly Weapons*]; *Coffman*; *Kennett*.

Armistice, occupation, recovery, and demobilization. *Harbord*; *OBUS*.

Retrospective. *Ayers*.

Sidebars. *NDB*; *JJPM*; *ACV Ency.*; Joseph Theodore Dickman, *The Great Crusade: A Narrative of the World War* (New York & London: D. Appleton and Company, 1927); Edward M. Coffman, *The Hilt of the Sword: The Career of Peyton C. March* (Madison, Milwaukee, and London: The University of Wisconsin Press, 1966); Peyton C. March, *The Nation At War* (Garden City, NY: Doubleday, Doran & Company, Inc., 1932); Donald Smythe, "The Pershing–March Conflict in World War I," *Parameters* (XI, No. 4); *Black Jack*; *OBUS*.

Index

Aircraft Production Board 83
Aisne-Marne campaign 70–71, 74
  initial plan of attack **72**
  operations of 1st and 2d Divisions 31, **73**
Alexander, Major General Robert 38, 40
Allen, Major General Henry T. 85
American Civil War 30
American Expeditionary Forces (AEF)
  Air Service 51, **51**, **52–53**, 55
    aces **75**
    aircraft 82–83
    De Havilland DH-4 82, 83, **83**
    Observation Squadron **54–55**
    Pursuit (Fighter) Squadron **53–54**
  Army Sanitary Schools, Langres **78**
  artillery 80–81
  black soldiers 12, 62
  casualties 6, 25, 41, 88
  command 20–23
  communication 23–26
  corps
    I Corps 11, 29, 30–31, **31**, 40
    III Corps 29
    V Corps 70
  demobilization 85, 87
  development 5–6
  divisions 32, **32**, **33–34**, 34
    1st 12, 13–14, 15, 17, 21, 22, 25, 34, **35–36**,
      36, 40–41, 65, 66–70, **84**, **85**, 87, **89**
    1st Expeditionary Division 9–10, 10
    26th "Yankee" 36, **37–38**, 38, 40–41, **40**
    41st 30
    42d 22
    77th "Metropolitan" 22, 38, **39**, 40,
      40–41
    92d "Buffalo" 40, 62
    93d 62
    depot 32
    importance of 27
    statistical comparisons between 40–41
  engineer regiments 60–61, **60**, **61**
    guidons 69
  field artillery brigades 45, **46–47**, 51
    1st 34, 65
    51st 36
    152d 38
  field artillery regiments (heavy) 45, **49**, **50**,
    51, 80
  field artillery regiments (light) 45, **48–49**,
    51, 69, 80
  field signal battalions **24–25**
  First Army 22, 29–30, **30**
    "famous colored band" **62**
    "G Staff" 28, 60
  G-2 intelligence section 6, **22**, **23**, 26
  General Headquarters, Chaumont 12, 20,
    27, 57–58
    organization 27–28, **29**
  infantry battalions **44**
  infantry brigades 41, **41**, **42**, 45
    1st 34

2d 34, 36, 66
51st 36
52d 36
153d 38
154th 38
infantry regiments **43–44**
  16th 17–18, 34, 36, 70
  18th 17–18, 34, 66, 67, 70, 71, **79**
  26th 17–18, 34, 66, 70
  28th 10, 17–18, 35, 65–66, 67, 70, **78**
infantry rifle companies **44–45**
intelligence 6, **22**, **23**, 26
Marine Corps 41
medical services 62
North Russia 62
officers 11–12, 15, 18
rail and truck transport 81–82
Services of Supply (SOS) 28, 51, 57–60, **58**,
  59, 81
Siberia 62
tactics 63–65
  aerial combat 74
  tank combat 74–75
tank battalions **57**
Tank Corps 55–57, **55**
theater of operations **16**
Tractor and Artillery School, St. Maur, Paris
  45
training 10
  artillery **45**, **49**
  divisional training areas **13**
  in France 12–15
  incompleteness of 65
  Pétain on 64
  schools in France 15–18
  in the US 11–12
trench mortar batteries **51**
weapons and equipment
  armored fighting vehicles 81
  automatic weapons 79–80
  Hotchkiss 8mm machine guns 78–79,
    79
  Schneider 155mm howitzers 80–81, **80**
  Springfield rifles 78
  uniforms and service kit 78
American Forces in France 62
American Forces in Germany 62, 85
Andrews, Brigadier General **28**
Argonne Forest 38, 40, 75
Armistice (November 11, 1918) 84–85
  American positions at **86**

Babcock, Private Carlisle **19**
Baker, Colonel Chauncey B. 9, 14, 56
Baker, Newton D. 7, **7**, 10, **19**, **21**
  career 19
Baker Board 21, 56, 79
Ballou, Brevet Major General Charles C. 62
Bell, Major General J. Franklin 11
Belleau Wood 64
Benét-Mercié machine guns 79

Biddle, Major General John 20
Bjornstad, Brigadier General Alfred W. 15
Black, Major General William M. **7**
Bliss, General Tasker Howard 20, **21**, 27, **82**,
  84
  career 21
Bolling, Major Raynal C. 82
Bourg 56, 57
Bovington, England 56
Braine, Lieutenant Elgin 56
Brenton, Private R.E. **80**
Bridges, General Tom **9**
Browning, John 79
Buck, Major General Beaumont B. **65**, 66, 70
Bullard, Major General Robert L. 15, 20, 36,
  36, 38, 64
Bundy, Major General Omar 11
Bureau of Aircraft Production 82
Bureau of Military Aeronautics 82
Butler, Colonel Smedley D. 85

Camp Colt, Pennsylvania 56
Camp Dix, New Jersey **88**
Camp Lee, Virginia 11
Camp Upton, New York 38, 41, 62
Campbell, 1st Lieutenant Douglas **75**
Cantigny, battle of (May 28, 1918) 64, 65–70,
  68, 74–75
Caserne de Damrémont 27
Castelnau, General Noel Marie Joseph Edward
  de Curières de 17
Charlevaux Mill 40
Château-Thierry 70
Chauchat light machine guns 79
Chaudun 70
Clemenceau, Georges 17
Coeuvres 70, **74**
Coffman, Edward 38
Coleman, 1st Lieutenant Wm. O. 69
Colored Officers Training Camp, Des Moines
  62
Colt .45 pistols 79
Colyer, Sergeant Wilbur 61
Compiègne Forest 70
Conner, Brigadier General Fox 9, 20, 25, **28**,
  89
Craig, Brigadier General Malin **23**, 30, 88
Cravançon Farm 71
Cullison, Lieutenant Colonel J.M. 67
Curtiss JN-4 training aircraft 82

Davis, Brigadier General **28**
Dawes, Charles G. 28
Dickman, Major General Joseph T. 20, 22, **23**,
  85
  career 23
Downer, Lieutenant Colonel John W. 69
Doyen, Brigadier General Charles A. 11
Drain, Major James A. 57
Drill, Small Arms and Field Service 14
Drum, Brigadier General Hugh 22

Edwards, Major General Clarence 36, 38, **38**
Eisenhower, Lieutenant Colonel Dwight 56
Eltinge, Brigadier General **28**
Ely, Major General Hanson 10, 66, 67
Enfield rifles 78–79
Escadrille Lafayette 74

Field Service Regulations, 1914 10, 63, 64
field signal projector lamp **26**
Fiske, Brigadier General Harold B. **11**, 12, 13–14, 15, 18, 20, **28**
Foch, Marshal Ferdinand 29, 36, 65, 84
Fokker, Anthony 74
Ford, Bert 38
Ford Motor Company 83
Fort Benjamin Harrison, Indiana 12
Fort Des Moines, Iowa 12
Fort Devens, Massachusetts 36
Fort Leavenworth, Kansas 6
Fort Sheridan, Illinois 12
Forsanz (French commander) 75
Foulois, Brigadier General Benjamin D. 29, 51
French Army
    XX Corps 70
    26th French Division, Chasseurs Alpins **5**
    training of AEF 12–15

Garrison, Lindley M. 19, 20
Garros, Roland 74
General Organization Project (GOP) 56
Germany, occupation of by US forces 85
Goethals, Major General George W. 59–60
Gowenlock, Major T.R. **84**
Graham, 1st Lieutenant John R. 71

Harbord, Major General James G. **19**, 20, 21, 28, 57, 59, 60, 62, **82**, 85
Hills, 2d Lieutenant E.E. 69
Hines, Brigadier General John L. 70, 88
Hoffman, Brigadier General Roy 62
Hotchkiss, Benjamin 79
House, Colonel Edward 84
howitzers 80–81, **80**
Huebner, Lieutenant Colonel Clarence Ralph 66, **66**

Infantry Drill Regulations, 1911 10, 63
influenza epidemic (1918) 88
Issoudun flying field **28**

Kenly, Major General William L. 82
Kernan, Major General Francis J. 59
King, Colonel Campbell **36**
Krag-Jörgensen rifles 78

Lane, Captain M.H. **84**
Langres 15, 56, 57
Lanham, Captain M.W. **85**
Laversine 70
Lawton, Major General Henry W. 36
Lewis, Isaac 79
"Liberty" engines 83
Liggett, Major General Hunter 11, 20, 21, 22, 30, 36, **38**, 40, **62**, 64
Line of Communications (LOC) 57
Logan, Major General John 5
Longavesne 70
Lorraine front **16**, 17

McAdoo, William 81
McAndrew, Colonel James A. 15
McAndrew, Major General James W. 18, 20, **28**, 36, 75
MacArthur, Colonel Douglas 11–12, 22
McGlachlin, Major General Edward F. 29, **84**, 85
McHenry, Private Herbert L. 11, 78, 79, 80
machine guns 79, **79**
Malone, Brigadier General Paul B. **10**, 12, 20
March, General Peyton Conway 20, **23**, 34, 56, 59
    career 23
Marr, Captain Kenneth **75**
Marshall, Brigadier General Francis C. **84**
Marshall, Lieutenant Colonel George C. 17, 20, 22, 25–26, 36, 60, 65, 66, 70, 75, 88
Marty, General (French Army) 85
Maxey, Lieutenant Colonel Robert J. 66
Maxim, Hiram 79
Meuse-Argonne campaign
    communications 25–26
    US offensive on (September 26, 1918) 40, 60, **77**
    use of tanks 75
Midvale Steel and Ordnance Company 81
Millett, Allan 65
Missy-aux-Bois ravine 71
Mitchell, Lieutenant Colonel William "Billy" 51
Moseley, Brigadier General George Van Horn **28**, 81

Nathness, Captain Albert 71
National Defense Act (1916) 7, 11, 27
National Defense Act (1920) 89
National Guard 11, 32, 36, 38
Nenninger, Timothy 23, 65
Neufchâteau 30
New York parade (September 10, 1919) **89**
Nolan, Brigadier General **28**

"open warfare" 63–64
Ottenfeld, Private Max 84, **87**
Overman Act (1918) 20

Packard Motor Car Company 83
Palmer, Lieutenant Colonel John McAuley 5, 27
Parker, Brigadier General Frank 22, 56, 70, **70**, **84**
Patch, Major Joseph Dorst 11, 70, 71, 79
Patrick, Major General Mason N. 51, **60**
Patton, Lieutenant Colonel George S. **14**, 56, 57, 75, 89
Pershing, General John J. **5**, **6**, **7**, **9**, **22**, **28**, **63**
    and the armistice 84
    at Cantigny 65
    career 6
    character 6, 20–21
    as commander-in-chief of AEF 8, 20–21
    on preparations for war 9
    reputation 88
    tactics 63–64
    on tanks 56
    on training 10, 14–15, 15–16, 18, 63
Pétain, Marshal Henri **22**, 29, 64, 84
pigeon couriers 25–26
Plattsburg Barracks, New York 12
Prince, Sergeant W.B. **23**

Pullen, Lieutenant Colonel Daniel 57
Punitive Expedition (1916) 34, 36, 82

Read, Major General George W. **64**
recruiting posters **25**
Rickenbacker, 1st Lieutenant E.V. **75**
Rockenbach, Brigadier General Samuel D. 56, **56**, 57, 75
Roosevelt, Lieutenant Quentin: grave of **74**
Roosevelt Jr., Lieutenant Colonel Theodore **84**
Roquencourt 70
Rozelle, Major George F. 67
Ryan, John D. 82, **82**

St. Mihiel campaign 29, 31, 60
    26th Division at 38
    Patton's use of armor at 57, 75, **76**
School of Aviation at Vineuil (Henri Farré) **17**
School of the Line 6
Scott, Major General Hugh L. 8, **8**, 10, 20
Sedan 22
Selective Service Act (1917) 7, 11
Sharp, William G. **7**
Shirey, Lieutenant Guy 36
Sibert, Major General William L. 17, 36
Soissons campaign 21–22, 25, 70–71, 74
Spanish–American War (1898) 30
Staff College, Fort Leavenworth 6
Standard Aero Corporation J-1 training aircraft 82
Summerall, Major General Charles P. 21–22, 65–66, 69, 70, **71**, 88
Supreme War Council 27, 84
Swanker, Sergeant **25**
Swinton, Sir Ernest 56

tables of organization and equipment (TO&E) 27
tanks
    Mark VIII "Liberty" 57
    Renault light **14**, **31**, 56
telegraph trailers **26**
Tours 57–58
trench warfare 63–64

Upton, Emory 5
US Army
    lessons learned from the war 88–89
    nature of 4–5, 7
    regulars 11, 32
    tactics 63
US Railroad Administration 81

Valdahon 12, 18
Vesle River 29, 38, 40, 70
Vickers Company 81
Vigneulles 38
The Volunteer Soldier in America (Logan) 5
Von Hindenburg (horse) **85**
Voris, Colonel A.C. **23**

War Department
    General Staff (WDGS) 6, 10, 27
    organization **20**
    War College Division 27
Wellborn, Colonel Ira C. 56
Western Front (1917) **4**
Whittlesey, Major Charles 40
Wilson, President Woodrow 7, **7**, 10, 81, 85
Wood, Leonard 9